"It's old news by now that evangelic: Barth with great appreciation. Not groundswell of interest in Barth am scholarly guild. For these readers, Ma ....as written a refreshingly concise, warmhearted, and plain-spoken biography of Barth that also serves as an introduction to his theology. Bravo!"

— JOHN WILSON
founding editor of *Education & Culture*

"In this warm introduction Mark Galli succinctly captures Barth's brilliance, his historical importance, and his intoxication with the gospel of Jesus Christ. Without shying away from the universalism question, Galli urges us to consider Barth's claims and what preaching a Christ-centered gospel with Barth might mean in a pluralistic world."

— JEFFREY Y. MCSWAIN
founder of Reality Ministries

"Galli's appreciative but critical posture makes this an ideal starting place for evangelicals (and others) who want to better understand Barth and his ongoing significance for Christian witness in the twenty-first century."

— JOHN R. FRANKE
author of *Barth for Armchair Theologians*

KARL BARTH

An Introductory Biography
for Evangelicals

MARK GALLI

William B. Eerdmans Publishing Company
Grand Rapids, Michigan

Wm. B. Eerdmans Publishing Co.
2140 Oak Industrial Drive NE, Grand Rapids, Michigan 49505
www.eerdmans.com

© 2017 Mark Galli
All rights reserved
Published 2017
Printed in the United States of America

26 25 24 23 22 21 20 19 18 17   1 2 3 4 5 6 7 8 9 10

ISBN 978-0-8028-6939-5

Library of Congress Cataloging-in-Publication Data

Names: Galli, Mark, author.
Title: Karl Barth : an introductory biography for evangelicals / Mark Galli.
Description: Grand Rapids : Eerdmans Publishing Co., 2017. |
   Includes bibliographical references and index.
Identifiers: LCCN 2017023581 | ISBN 9780802869395 (pbk. : alk. paper)
Subjects: LCSH: Barth, Karl, 1886-1968.
Classification: LCC BX4827.B3 G355 2017 | DDC 230/.044092—dc23
   LC record available at https://lccn.loc.gov/2017023581

To my friends in Brewing Theology,
who, with a mug in one hand and a book in the other,
have helped me do theology more faithfully

Contents

Introduction

You know you're dealing with an unusual theologian when he compares himself to a whale. Or was it an elephant?

On Christmas Eve 1952, Karl Barth wrote a letter to his theological nemesis Rudolf Bultmann, the scholar famous for his attempt to "demythologize" the New Testament. They had engaged in theological debate for years, with little quarter given by either. Barth compared the two of them to a whale and an elephant: "It is all for nothing that one sends his spout of water high in the air. It is all for nothing that the other moves its trunk now in friendship and now in threat."[1]

So, was Barth the elephant or the whale? I suspect most readers, if they are like my toddler son, think of him as an elephant. As my wife and I walked and pushed his stroller through the local zoo many years ago, we excitedly pointed out each animal he had been seeing in his picture books—chimpanzee, lion, gnu, and so forth. When we approached the elephant enclosure, I hurriedly pushed Luke's stroller up close, and just as I was about to say, "Luke, look, an elephant!" he let out a terrific scream and began pulling at the stroller straps to escape. Needless to say, we made a hasty retreat. I suddenly realized that, for my son, the sheer size of the elephant was not so much impressive as frightening.

Such is the reaction of many who, curious about Barth, stroll up to take a look. We flip through the nearly 9,000 pages of the Church

Dogmatics, read a passage or two of his dense prose, and run for our theological lives.

We're curious, because we've heard that Barth was an immense influence. He saved orthodoxy from the ravages of liberal theology, rescued the Bible from religious relativism, rediscovered the gospel in all its power and splendor, and put Jesus Christ back at the center of the church's preaching. Like an elephant in a china shop (to alter the image), Barth furiously butted against fine and delicate conclusions of nineteenth-century theology, which came crashing to the floor. Or, as one theologian put it, Barth's *Epistle to the Romans* "fell like a bombshell on the playground of theologians."[2]

Such analogies fall short, because Barth did more than demolish. He was also a master builder, who not only razed the theological Tower of Babel of his era, but in its place constructed from the ground up a towering cathedral made of Calvin and Luther, Augustine and Paul, and of course Karl Barth. But its structure was most deeply shaped by the Bible, and for this reason his theology is not something that will ever be destroyed. Challenged, debated, altered, yes—but it simply cannot be dismissed. It has changed the cityscape of modern theology, and more importantly, the church-scape of the twentieth and twenty-first centuries. No serious theologian can venture into the streets of this city without first taking a tour of Barth's cathedral.

Theological Genius

"Karl Barth is the greatest theological genius that has appeared on the scene for centuries." He "has, in fact, so changed the whole landscape of theology, evangelical and Roman alike, that the other great theologians of modern times appear in comparison rather like jobbing gardeners." So wrote the eminent theologian Thomas F. Torrance in 1962, who was no jobbing gardener himself.[3]

This judgment is partly due to Barth's tremendous output.

Barth is best known for his fourteen-volume *Church Dogmatics*. It is to be sure a work of staggering genius—as Torrance said of just one of the volumes (IV): it "surely constitutes the most powerful work on the doctrine of atoning reconciliation ever written."[4] But it is also a work twice as long as that of another elephant of a theologian, Thomas Aquinas's *Summa theologiae*. Barth called his work his Moby Dick,[5] referring to the great white whale that the monomaniacal Ahab pursued in Herman Melville's famous novel. The *Dogmatics* alone would be a lifetime achievement for any theologian, except that Barth also wrote other books, gave addresses at conferences, preached sermons, and wrote letters.

It was a kind of divine madness that overtook Barth after his conversion from liberalism. Melville wrote that the white whale swam before Ahab "as the monomaniac incarnation of all those malicious agencies which some deep men feel eating in them."[6] Similarly, when Barth looked at theology in his day, he saw the "monomaniac" spirit of liberalism, with its relentless framing of the Christian faith in terms of what human beings feel and experience, not what God has done in Christ. For Barth liberalism became his white whale; he was a monomaniacal Captain Ahab in his relentless pursuit of liberalism's destruction, an obsessive captain on the high seas of theology.

I don't know exactly what Torrance meant when he called Barth a genius, but if I were to outline the seven traits of theological genius, I would pick these (with the caveat that Barth would hate being described as such!).

1. The theological genius must be a voracious reader. Since theology is about God and his creation, its subject is *everything*. He must be aware of the full sweep of Christian theology, from Paul, to Justin, to Tertullian, to Irenaeus, to Athanasius, to Augustine, to Anselm, to Aquinas, to Calvin, to Luther, to Wesley, to Edwards, to Schleiermacher, to Harnack—to name a few!

Then there's related reading in literature, philosophy, science, and so forth.

2. The theological genius must, therefore, be able to read quickly. Some of us are slow and plodding readers, which limits our ability to gain an appreciation of the depth and breadth of the Christian tradition. The theological genius is able to absorb lots of material quickly.

3. Some fortunate people can read vast amounts of material quickly, and even gobble a book a day, no matter the subject. But in conversing with them, one does not perceive that the books have made a deep impression on them. Or they may not have engaged the books' arguments in a thoughtful way. The theological genius can not only read quickly but also engage the material he is reading.

4. The theological genius will also publicly react to what he has read, usually in lectures, articles, and books. He inwardly processes the material he has absorbed and pondered and then can articulate his views in ways others find thoughtful and fresh.

5. The theological genius will, therefore, have a tremendous work ethic. He will be able to give himself to the tasks of reading, writing, and lecturing from early morning to late at night. He will be willing to work on his 8 a.m. lecture until 3 or 4 that morning to make sure he has it right. He will forgo trips to exotic lands and lucrative speaking opportunities and book contracts that would distract him from the task at hand. He will do this not only for weeks on end, but for a lifetime.

6. The theological genius will have something positive to add to our theological knowledge. It doesn't take a genius to deconstruct what is wrong with the current theological scene. It takes a person of extraordinary ability to construct something positive.

7. The theological genius will not merely add a positive contribution but will shape his era, if not the theological conversation, for centuries to come.

Needless to say, Karl Barth fit all these descriptions, as we will see as this book unfolds.

Aims of This Book

Barth's legacy is so huge, his insights so rich, his ruminations so profound, his influence so powerful that it is impossible to take it all in. I make no claim to having read all the *Church Dogmatics*, all of his correspondence, all of the secondary literature. Like my son, I've found myself at times running from the massive output of Barth and Barthian scholars.

Nor do I try to give a detailed, balanced, or complete view of his life. The crucial chapters in his life came in the early decades of the twentieth century. It was his commentary on Romans that catapulted Barth onto the scene and sent shockwaves through church and academy; it is in this commentary, despite its excesses, that we first find themes that profoundly shaped his later theology. More interesting to me is that it contains themes that I believe are particularly relevant to evangelicalism today. So I spend some space on this monumental book.

I also spend considerable space on Barth's reaction to Hitler and the rise of National Socialism in 1930s Germany. I want readers to understand the nature of the temptation facing the German church in this era. This is the only way to grasp what Barth was driving at in the Barmen Declaration. We have to move beyond the cartoonish summaries (evil Hitler, cowardly church, prophetic Barth) if we are going to learn from this era.

When it comes to the *Church Dogmatics*, I do not even attempt a summary of this great work. Other introductory biographies—such as the ones by John Franke and Densil Morgan and John Webster—do this better than I ever could. Instead, I focus on two themes from the *Dogmatics* and try to show how one evangelical non-scholar mines Barth's insights to shape his theology. I want to show that

Barth's theology is very much worth wrestling with, even when in the end you have to disagree at one point or another.

I believe that talk about Barth is not nearly as interesting as Barth's talk. So the biography is littered with quotations from his letters, lectures, and books. No writer can give a flavor of Barth's approach to life and theology better than Barth himself.

For the shape of his life, I have been deeply dependent on the work of Eberhard Busch. Busch was Barth's last assistant, and he spent a considerable part of his life gathering Barth's letters and occasional writings into books that could be mined by future scholars. I've been particularly grateful for his *Karl Barth: His Life from Letters and Autobiographical Texts*. In many parts of this book I am doing little more than condensing Busch's fine work for my own ends.

Still, I have found occasional fresh insights and information in several popular theological summaries, as well as in deeper theological explorations by great Barth scholars such as George Hunsinger and Bruce McCormack. In addition, snippets have been gleaned from Barth's introductions to various volumes of his *Dogmatics*, as well as other books. I've kept endnotes to a minimum since I'm not intending a fresh work of scholarship but a readable narrative based on the scholarship that has gone before me. Still, at the end, I have listed all the books that have helped me in one way or another in the course of my writing. I look forward to the day when a full biography is published, grounded especially in German sources that I cannot access. But until then, I trust this little volume will be useful.

The two themes I've picked from the *Church Dogmatics* have shaped my thinking as a pastor, religion journalist, and amateur theologian. I want to show how Barth's theology can be read, absorbed, and reshaped by one's own convictions to enlarge one's understanding of Jesus Christ as revealed in Scripture. I trust you'll see that I love Karl Barth not because I always agree with him, but because he forces me to think more faithfully and encourages me to love God more fervently.

At the end of the book, I conclude with a chapter that explores some of Barth's early themes and juxtapose them with some currents in evangelical thought and life. This is an attempt to use Barth to help evangelicals think about our life together as evangelicals. From a historical perspective, this is a dangerous enterprise! For the liberalism that I believe tempts American evangelicalism today is not exactly the liberalism that permeated nineteenth-century Europe. But I believe there are enough similarities to prompt some soul-searching and conversation.

The Joy of Barth

Like novelist John Updike, I've especially appreciated Barth's "frank supernaturalism." It's the Barthian theme that has most attracted me, and it's the main reason I decided to write a biography that, I trust, will entice others to read Barth.

As Updike put it, Barth says "with resounding definiteness and learning what I needed to hear . . . that it really *was* so, that there was something within us that would not die, and we live by faith alone." In fact, Updike seriously misreads Barth here. It's not that there is "something within us" that will not die, but that the God *outside us* makes it possible for us—all of us, not just some of us— to live, now and forever. I think what Updike senses is that Barth communicates the hope of the gospel like few other theologians. Updike put it this way: "After one has conquered . . . existential terror with Barth's help, then one is able to open to the world again. He certainly was very open to the world. Wonderfully alive and relaxed, as a man."[7]

To be sure, Barth has his share of personal and theological flaws, but he remains an infectious writer, a man whose thinking and personality were "wonderfully alive." Evangelicals rightly question his doctrine of Scripture, but those who do read him are, paradoxically, driven time and again back to their Bibles. Because his theology is so grounded in Scripture, Barth is able as few can to remind us of the height, breadth, and depth of God's love in Jesus Christ. The more I read him, the more I am able to engage the world in Christ's name with joy and confidence.

As editor in chief of *Christianity Today*, I try to be sensitive to the character and nuances of American evangelicalism. I recognize that, although Barth now has a strong following among younger evangelical theologians, he has been held in suspicion by most our tribe. And for good reason. He was sometimes careless in his expression, and frankly he taught some things that create more problems than they solve.

The automobile, when it was invented, was viewed by many as a dangerous, troublesome, "newfangled contraption," and many still preferred the relative safety and familiarity of the horse and buggy. No question that Barth's theology can be dangerous at times, that it sometimes goes too fast for its own good. Then again, if you want to travel the vast country of God's grace and get a sweeping view of the wonder of God's mercy in Jesus Christ, there are few theologians better equipped to help you travel those exquisite highways.

CHAPTER 1

An Uneasy Relationship

There are a thousand subtle ways that we can attack Barthianism and Neo-Orthodoxy without actually calling it by name. Let us pray that God will give us the wisdom of a Solomon.

—Billy Graham, in a letter to Carl Henry, October 1956

These people have already had their so-called orthodoxy for a long time. They are closed to anything else, they will cling to it at all costs, and they can adopt toward me only the role of prosecuting attorneys.

—Karl Barth, in response to three evangelical theologians who queried him about his theology, June 1960

Evangelicals love Dietrich Bonhoeffer. His classics *Cost of Discipleship* and *Life Together* are perennial favorites for personal and small group study as well as homiletic quotes. Even as we debate the ethics of Bonhoeffer's participation in an assassination plot against Adolf Hitler, we admire his moral and physical courage in the face of the great evil of his day. So if we like Bonhoeffer so much, why do we distrust the theologian whom Bonhoeffer admired more than any other?

Bonhoeffer biographer Clifford Green says that Barth was "the only theologian to whom [Bonhoeffer] gave real authority in his work."[1] Bonhoeffer was critical of Barth at points, but he emphasized that any critique he made came "from inside and not outside the Barthian movement."[2] When Bonhoeffer spent some time at Union Theological Seminary in New York in 1930, he was, according to theologian John Baillie (a student at Union at the time), "the most convinced disciple of Dr. Barth that had appeared among us up to that time, and withal as stout an opponent of liberalism as had ever come my way."[3]

Bonhoeffer relished Barth's return to "the tradition of Paul, Luther, Kierkegaard . . . the tradition of genuine Christian thinking" and the recovery of "the world of biblical thinking." Barth, said Bonhoeffer, set aside mere "religious thinking" for thinking grounded in "the Word of God . . . , the revelation straight from above, from outside of man, according to the justification of the sinner by grace."[4]

Barth also shared Bonhoeffer's early distrust of Adolf Hitler, long before most of their theological and pastoral colleagues sniffed out the dangers of fascism. Barth did not pay for his opposition with his life, but he was fired from his German university and forced to return to Switzerland. In this episode, Bonhoeffer is remembered for the life he gave to thwart Hitler, but Barth is remembered for the theology—the Barmen Declaration—that undergirded Christian efforts to resist Nazi idolatry.

So Barth, like Bonhoeffer, was a champion of orthodox theology who grounded his theology on the Word of God, who recovered the priority of grace, who stood courageous against the great evil of his day—and yet, he is either ignored or dismissed by evangelicals. There are theological concerns to be reckoned with, to be sure. But many theological concerns we have about Barth could easily be directed at Bonhoeffer. For example, though both mined the riches of the Bible to form their theology, neither held to the inerrancy of Scripture.

So what has caused such a deep distrust of Barth among evangelicals in particular?

The Early Origins of Evangelicalism

The problem began before Barth ever heard of American evangelicals and American evangelicals of Barth. Barth first encountered evangelical-like people in European Pietism, a first cousin to American evangelicalism. We will see that Barth learned something of Pietism from his immediate family and its heritage. But there remained a lot about Pietism that repelled Barth.

Pietism was a movement that emerged in the late 1600s, started by Lutheran pastor Philipp Jakob Spener. Born in 1635 in Ribeauvillé in Upper Alsace, Spener was deeply influenced by a devout godmother and eventually studied theology at Strasbourg, where practical versus doctrinal Christianity was the order of the day. After a year in Geneva, where he became taken with the city's strict morality, he took a pastorate in Frankfurt. He strove to create a church known more for devotion than for strict Lutheran orthodoxy.

In 1675 Spener published *Pia desideria* or *Earnest Desire for a Reform of the True Evangelical Church*. In it he argued for church reform and proposed, among other things, intense study of the Bible in small groups (what he called "little churches within the church"), a focus on practicing (not just believing) the faith, an emphasis on devotional life, and a more direct and personal preaching and teaching style.

While many Lutheran theologians and pastors rejected Spener, his ideas soon gained a large following. After his death in 1705, the movement was guided by August Hermann Francke, the founder of a famous orphanage at Halle. Another key development was the revival that blossomed among Moravians at the village of Herrnhut in late 1727, led by Count von Zinzendorf, Spener's godson and a pupil in the Halle School for Young Noblemen. Out of this emerged the first Protestant overseas missions, which made courageous forays into the West Indies (1732), into Greenland (1733), and among North American Indians (1735).

Pietism's emphasis on the need for spiritual rebirth and moral separation from the world led to excesses. For example, in some places the new birth was not considered genuine unless it was preceded by anguished spiritual torment and dramatic repentance. In addition, many Pietists drifted into legalism, banning all worldly amusements—dancing, public games, and the theater.

But in its healthy and typical forms, Pietism was a powerful antidote to the day's prevailing formalism. The devotion John Wesley found in Pietistic literature forced him to question the depth of his Anglican faith. His famous conversion—when he experienced his heart being "strangely warmed" after hearing a reading of Luther's preface to his commentary on Romans—transformed his ministry. The preaching of the new birth by him and George Whitefield ignited the Great Awakening in Britain and America. That revival can be said to be the start of American and British evangelicalism. There remains to this day a striking family resemblance between evangelicalism and Pietism.

Barth and the European "Evangelicals"

The Pietists of Barth's day had a mixed reaction to Barth. Some appreciated his rediscovery of the Bible and his emphasis on the dynamic power of the preached word. His skewering of nineteenth-century liberalism was another plus, for liberalism had long rejected and mocked Pietism. But in the end, Barth was no Pietist, as Barth made abundantly clear.

For Barth it wasn't merely a matter of theology. The sort of person Pietism often produced left him cold. As he said in an early sermon, he was put off by the Pietists' "unpleasant habit of smelling and sniffing at their fellow human beings to find out if they are converted" and their "unnatural rules about what we call 'Christian' and 'non-Christian.'"[5] Or, as he put it in another sermon, "Blessed are those who know they are not pious! . . . They are the people of God because they know they are not."[6]

Barth didn't deny that Pietism had some legitimate concerns

and goals. Take its desire to be separate from the world: this reflected Pietists' understanding that, in the end, God calls his people to an utterly new existence in Christ. The problem, Barth said, was that Pietists thought significant transformation could be achieved in this life, which all too naturally led them to believe that such could be produced mechanically. Instead, Barth believed that redemption would come only as a gift when Christ returned.

To be fair, many Pietists recognized the temptation of self-righteousness. Thus many argued that humility—understanding that we cannot be redeemed except by God's power—was a prerequisite to spiritual growth. But even in this Barth was troubled, for he saw a subtle but insidious injection of human will:

> Not only the direct path from humanity to God but even the negation of such paths is not a way to reach God. Even humility, even every form of self-denial, even the knowledge of having no claim to God's grace does not give me any claim to it. So even when I renounce my own "possessing," I do not have God; rather I am still focusing on myself.[7]

It wasn't just the temptation to legalism but its relentless focus on the individual that Barth found troubling. In one early lecture, he said,

> Can one read or hear read even as much as two chapters from the Bible and still with good conscience say, God's word went forth to humanity, his mandate guided history from Abraham to Christ, the Holy Spirit descended in tongues of fire upon the apostles at Pentecost, a Saul became a Paul and traveled over land and sea—all in order that here and there specimens of men like you and me might be "converted," find inner "peace," and by a redeeming death go some day to "heaven." Is that all? Is that all of God and his new world, of the meaning of the Bible, of the content of the contents?[8]

5

American Evangelical Reaction to Barth

Since the blood of Pietism runs thick in modern evangelicalism, there is little doubt that Barth would have had similar concerns about much of American evangelicalism. But American evangelicalism is a strange mix of Pietism and rationalism, and Barth had little sympathy with either. It did not help matters that the first major evangelical interpreter of Barth (a rationalist) got him wrong.

In 1946, Cornelius Van Til, professor of theology at Westminster Seminary in Pennsylvania, published his first critique in *The New Modernism: An Appraisal of the Theology of Barth and Brunner*. He returned to Barth time and again, especially in *Christianity and Barthianism* (1962) and *Karl Barth and Evangelicalism* (1964).

Van Til made the surprising claim—given Barth's actual writings—that Barth's theology "is the diametric opposite of a theology that is based on a finished revelation of God in history." The reason Barth's theology sounds like a champion of traditional orthodoxy, argued Van Til, is that it contains many "verbal similarities to historic Protestantism." But Van Til believed Barth's theology was, "in effect, a denial of it." In the end, Van Til said Barth was a champion of the "would-be autonomous man."[9]

To construe Barth in this way is "difficult in the extreme," says former Wheaton theologian Kevin Vanhoozer.[10] Everybody else sees that Barth rediscovered the priority of God in theology. But the damage had been done, and a generation of conservative theologians who looked to Van Til—because he was, in fact, an otherwise creative and thoughtful philosopher and theologian—continued to hold Barth at arm's length.

We see this played out on a popular level in the founding of *Christianity Today*. The magazine was conceived by its creator, Billy Graham, as an antidote to liberalism and as a means of championing evangelicalism. When Graham—who represents the Pietist strain—wrote Carl Henry, the first editor, critiquing the first issue of the magazine, he made it clear that Barth and the movement he represented, Neo-Orthodoxy, needed to be confronted, however subtly:

> Now, Carl, one other point, I believe we are going to make a serious mistake if at first we drive a wedge between evangelicals and Barthians. What we want to do is to win the Barthian and the Neo-Orthodox to a more evangelical position, but if we use the terms Barthian and Neo-Orthodox in criticism, I feel it is going to be a red flag that will drive them away. There are a thousand subtle ways that we can attack Barthianism and Neo-Orthodoxy without actually calling it by name. Let us pray that God will give us the wisdom of a Solomon and the ability to be wise as serpents and harmless as doves.[11]

Despite Graham's desire that a wedge not be driven, it was driven even deeper by Carl Henry himself, especially in his own theological works. A few years after its founding, Christianity Today invited Van Til and two other theologians to submit questions to Barth, who was planning a trip to America. The questions were delivered through Geoffrey Bromiley, translator of Barth's Dogmatics, who had a personal relationship with Barth.

Barth's reply suggests the tone of the query as well as Barth's imperious disgust with his interlocutors:

> These people have already had their so-called orthodoxy for a long time. They are closed to anything else, they will cling to it at all costs, and they can adopt toward me only the role of prosecuting attorneys, trying to establish whether what I represent agrees or disagrees with their orthodoxy, in which I for my part have no interest! None of their questions leaves me with the impression that they want to seek with me the truth that is greater than all of us. They take the stance of those who happily possess it already and who hope to enhance their happiness by succeeding in proving to themselves and the world that I do not

share this happiness. Indeed they have long since decided and publicly proclaimed that I am a heretic, possibly (van Til) the worst heretic of all time.[12]

The Turn to Barth

The fact that Bromiley, a conservative Reformed theologian at Fuller Theological Seminary, had given himself to the monumental task of translating Barth's *Church Dogmatics* for the English-speaking world suggests that a shift was already taking place in evangelicalism. In fact, a number of rising evangelical theologians of the day had either studied under Barth or were indebted to his theological insights—scholars such as Paul Jewett, Bernard Ramm, and Donald Bloesch.

But as recently as the late 1990s, Barth was still considered theologically suspect. I was editor of *Christian History* at the time, a magazine that was then owned by *Christianity Today*. Every issue of the popular church history magazine was thematic, and I suggested to my superior that we publish an issue on Karl Barth. He rejected the idea, saying that many if not most of the readers did not consider Barth an orthodox Christian. I had been theologically educated at Fuller Seminary in the 1970s, where many of the professors had engaged Barth constructively; one well-respected theologian, Ray Anderson, was deeply influenced by Barthian theology. So I was a little taken aback by my superior's judgment, but I soon recognized that he knew evangelicalism of the time better than I did.

With the turn of the millennium, things have turned a corner. Today one of the leading Barthians in the world, Bruce McCormack of Princeton Theological Seminary, while still distancing himself in some ways from the movement, identifies himself as an evangelical. And the ranks of evangelical scholars who have imbibed Barth deeply and believe he has a great deal to offer—even when they have serious disagreements with him—include Alister Mc-

Grath, Timothy George, Kevin Vanhoozer, and John Franke. Even Reformed theologian Michael Horton, who has some severe criticisms of Barth to offer, nonetheless acknowledges the debt we owe him: Barth's work represents a "Copernican revolution in the history of modern theology" in opposing the human-centered theology of neo-Protestantism and replacing it with "a thoroughgoing theocentricism that threw the light once again on divine initiative." While Horton challenges Barth's doctrine of the Word of God, he concludes that, when it comes to the priority of Scripture over the church or culture, "we are one."[13]

Today, evangelical theologians of every stripe agree that, while Barth may need to be corrected in a number of ways, no theologian can do work without understanding Barth. Even Barth's severe critics, such as William Evans at Erskine Seminary, recognize that "the temptation to enroll Barth in the cause of contemporary theological programs remains strong, especially on the more conservative end of the mainline theological spectrum."[14]

Barth in the Evangelical Trenches

Barth, then, is a force to contend with, and not merely in the rare climes of academic theology. The fact that an increasing number of evangelical theologians are examining Barth and mining him for positive contributions means that it is only a matter of time before Barthian theology, however chastened and revised, will make its way down into the pulpit and pews of evangelical churches and into the ministry of parachurch organizations. When that happens, it can lead to inspiration and devotion—as Bonhoeffer has done for us. But if we don't have a fuller understanding of Barth, it will only produce consternation and confusion—as one incident a few years back suggests.

Young Life is an evangelistic ministry that targets teens, mostly high school students, and, according to its website, offers seven hundred Young Life club meetings in over three hundred cities worldwide, with 39,000 volunteers and staff, reaching over a million junior and senior high youth each year. In late 2007, Young Life senior leaders issued a list of "Non-Negotiables" that Young Life staff needed to affirm. In a letter that accompanied the Non-Negotiables, Young Life president Denny Rydberg said the organization was concerned that the mission "not drift from our biblical and historical roots."

Terry Swenson, Young Life vice president of communications, explained the need for written Non-Negotiables: "As we grow, the need for a way to talk with one another about this important issue has come up. And the paper really is an attempt to guide and train and help folks prepare as they proclaim the gospel."

An organization does not issue a Non-Negotiables statement unless it feels that the non-negotiables are being negotiated. In this case, the cause was a paper circulated by Jeff McSwain, who at the time was a Young Life area director for Durham and Chapel Hill, North Carolina. In his paper, McSwain took issue with Young Life's "sin talks," where leaders explain that "God is holy and pure and we are impure." He was concerned that, in saying "We've broken the law and someone needs to pay," Young Life speakers were sounding more Unitarian than Trinitarian, because they were drawing a sharp contrast between the holy God and the incarnated Son who "actually became sin." Instead, McSwain wanted to mine Young Life's trademark contact-evangelistic strategy—incarnational friendship. But he felt that the messages of intrinsic separation from God introduced "serious confusion into the hearts of the kids who we love."

To the contrary, wrote McSwain, "I can go into the realm of the most lost, furthest-out kids, knowing something that is true about them before they do. They are lost children of God; people can't be lost unless they have a home!"

McSwain argued that the Non-Negotiables took an approach resembling Campus Crusade for Christ's "Four Spiritual Laws."

Talks begin with the person of Jesus Christ, but from there they move on to the reality and consequences of sin before presenting the crucifixion and resurrection of Christ. Talks end with an invitation to believe, become a disciple of Jesus, and publicly proclaim faith. To put it simply, the overall approach of Young Life is: *if* you repent, Jesus will forgive. McSwain's approach is: *because* we are already forgiven, we can repent.

Driving McSwain's concern was a theology deeply influenced by the late Scottish theologian Thomas Torrance (and to some degree his brother James) and Torrance's theological mentor Karl Barth. Both Thomas Torrance and Barth sought to redefine traditional Calvinism by arguing that God has a marriage-like relationship with the world—as opposed to a merely legal relationship that demands repentance before God will fully accept us.

Like other Reformed theologians, McSwain believes that true repentance is a gift from God—something the Non-Negotiables document seems to affirm when it says that "our response of repentance is only evidence of our change of heart, not the reason for our salvation." But McSwain and his friends argued that another phrase in the Non-Negotiables—"We believe that only in responding in faith and repentance can Jesus' removal of sin and the imparting of life begin"—amounts to a denial of the first statement. Some called it "insidious 'works righteousness' that is alien to the sovereign love and grace of God in Christ at work through the Holy Spirit."[15]

This is not the place to debate the merits of the argument between McSwain and Young Life, or to defend one or the other for subsequent events (McSwain was in fact fired and started his own youth ministry organization). In some ways, their argument is a perennial one in evangelicalism, one that often divides Reformed and Arminian evangelicals. But in this case, McSwain's Reformed views were deeply influenced by his reading of Barth and one of Barth's most influential disciples. In some ways, theirs is a Reformed theology on steroids, pushing hard on the priority of God's gracious action in Jesus Christ.

The larger point is this: Barth's theology (and that of his Scottish disciples, the Torrance brothers) will increasingly make its way into grassroots evangelicalism. This is going to alarm some and encourage others. In either case, evangelicals need to understand what in fact Barth does and does not teach so that, as we wrestle with each other over issues he raises, we can do so intelligently and charitably.

I believe that if we can be as charitable toward Barth as we have been toward Bonhoeffer, despite the questions and concerns Barth's theology raises, we will find in his insights a source of inspiration that can also help us wisely bear the cost of discipleship in these trying times.

CHAPTER 2

The Fighter

Today I did a good deal of bashing up and got bashed up by plenty of people myself.

—Karl Barth, age twelve, diary entry

Karl Barth was a fighter from day one, May 10, 1886, when he mightily resisted coming into the world. The birth seems to have been a difficult one for his mother, but it also did a number on Karl. An aunt said the new boy looked "quite terrible."

It was just the beginning of his turbulent boyhood.[1]

A Pious Family

It's not that Karl was born into a social setting that encouraged rebellion. He had a good pedigree and was nurtured in a loving home. He was the eldest child of a middle-class, conservative Swiss family, who lived in Basel at the time of his birth. His mother, Anna, was the daughter of a pastor and came from a family that included many pastors and professors. His father, Fritz, had earned a theology degree and was a teacher at the College of Preachers in Basel.

When Karl was three, the family moved to Berne so his father could take up a post teaching in the university. Fritz was an advocate of what was then called "positive theology," what we might describe as moderately conservative and warm Protestantism. He had been deeply influenced by Pietism, as was his wife. Both families came from a long line of warmly devout Christians. Karl's great-great-grandfather was Johannes Burkhardt, founder of the Society of Christianity and a good friend of the Herrnhut community, a hotbed of Pietism. Karl would later describe Burkhardt as a Pietist who believed not in doctrine "but in the Scriptures, existing in a living relationship to the living Lord Jesus Christ." Thus he was a "joyous Pietist." Karl's family tree also included Hieronymus Annoni, "father of Basel's Pietism," who knew Zinzendorf and the Pietists of Halle.

Fritz had a Pietist streak of his own. He called his conversion a "new birth" that ushered in "the beginning of new life in man," transforming him at his deepest roots, giving him an enduring "personal contact with Jesus." This was for him "the most wonderful and glorious of all God's works." Consequently, he believed Paul's description in Romans 7—where Paul wrestles with sin, unable to do the good because of his resistant flesh—to be a description of life before conversion. But once one has experienced "God as our God," one is "equipped for fruitful service by the power of God's Spirit."

So, while Fritz recognized the role of doctrine in the Christian faith, genuine, heart-felt spiritual experience was even more central. Orthodoxy too easily became an "ossification of church life." Too fierce a commitment to orthodoxy would undermine Christian faith.

Fritz was not indifferent to or unaware of the temptations to legalism or enthusiasm among Pietists. But he believed four positive features more than outweighed the negatives: (1) the priority of life over doctrine, (2) the need for spiritual birth, (3) the close connection between saving faith and the ensuing life of faith, and (4) the emphasis on the coming kingdom of God.[2]

The Martial Barth

Karl was soon joined by two brothers and two sisters (one of whom died of diphtheria in childhood). Barth later admitted that he did not always use his position as the eldest sibling rightly, that he not only was bossy but often used his siblings for his own purposes and jokes. "The consequence," he said, "was that my brothers, in particular, bore a grudge against me all through their lives."

For Fritz Barth, the responsibility of teaching theology was no match for the challenges of raising "Karli." In his diary, he noted that he had occasion to "beat" his son, a customary discipline of the day. But Karl didn't appear to resent his father as a result. All his life, he spoke of him only with the deepest respect. And he remained deeply attached to his mother, though he later said she brought him up too strictly. (In reaction, Karl later admitted, he became a very lenient father himself.)

All in all, he was raised in a loving family. Fritz often wrestled with his boys after lunch. And most of the discipline in the home was typical for the day and hardly abusive. His mother would lay down the law with a shaking of her head, or just silence. His father would often try to put things right with good advice. If his children were squabbling, he might raise his finger toward them and quote Scripture: "Behold how good and a joyful thing it is, brethren, to dwell in unity!" His mother would say in exasperation, "We need to take one of them and beat the others with it!"

So it was not poor parenting or a difficult environment but something in his genes that made Karl a fighter. The boy needed firmness, to say the least. All through childhood he said he "lived and dreamed of military exploits." He later said he would never forget the first book he read on war (and which he kept on his shelves for years), Christian Niemeyer's *A Book of Heroes: A Memorial of the Great Deeds of Wars of Liberation*. It contained, in Barth's words, a "bloodthirsty account of the wars against Bonaparte, whom it could not condemn too severely." In those days, he also said he read a bound copy of a magazine from the war years of 1870–71, which prominently featured "Bavarians swinging clubs and 'Turkos' in retreat." Later, he followed with great interest China's war with Japan in 1895 and, "like any boy, I delighted in the victory of the lesser power over the greater." In 1897, King Chulalongkorn of Bangkok visited Berne, escorted through the city by Swiss Dragoons, and Barth was so excited by the event that he worked up a fever and had to be put to bed!

He really meant it when he said he "lived" military exploits. Not only would he and his brothers play with toy soldiers for hours on end, but Karl got into his fair share of fist fights. For a time, he was part of a kind of street gang that provoked fights between his classmates and the City Grammar School, as well as between the sons of aristocratic families of Berne and boys from impoverished immigrant homes. A diary entry when he was twelve proudly reads, "Today I did a good deal of bashing up and got bashed up by plenty of people myself."

As one can imagine, school for such a boy was not exactly a high priority. He said he "tolerated the offerings and the demands of the lower school and the upper school as an inevitable cross I had to bear." He despised math and the natural sciences, but he was taken with history, particularly essay writing. When it came to his favorite subject, he was always at the top of his class. But overall he admitted that he behaved badly in school and received regular punishments and detentions.

Resolved to Become a Theologian

Slowly something resembling maturity and Christian faith began to take form in the boy—without necessarily subduing that martial spirit. It began, he later recollected, with the singing of children's hymns, Basel-German children's songs that had been written by theologian Abel Burckhardt. Though not imbued with deep theology, these songs, Barth said, gave him his first theological education:

> What made an indelible impression on me was the homely self-assurance with which these unpretentious verses spoke of the events of Christmas, Palm Sunday, Good Friday, Easter, Ascension, Pentecost, as though they could have taken place that very morning in Basel or nearby, like any other exciting event. History? Doctrine? Dogma? Myth? No! It was all things actually taking place. You could see everything for yourself and listen to it and take it to heart by hearing one of these songs sung in the language you were hearing elsewhere and beginning to speak, and you could join in the song yourself. Holding your mother's hand you went to the stable in Bethlehem, along the streets of Jerusalem, into which the savior was making his entry, hailed by children of your own age. You climbed the grim hill of Golgotha and walked in Joseph's garden at daybreak.

He said that, indeed, this was all very naïve, but "perhaps the deepest wisdom, with its fullest force, lies in naivety, and this kind of wisdom, once gained, can carry a man over whole oceans of historicism and anti-historicism, mysticism and rationalism, orthodoxy, liberalism and existentialism."[3]

Music was another steadying factor. He learned violin as a boy, and he acquired a "reasonable degree of competence" and played in the school orchestra. Still, he much preferred singing and developed a rich baritone voice.

When he was as young as five or six, he heard something that would shape his musical tastes for the rest of his life. His father was playing Mozart on the piano, and when he began playing some bars from Mozart's opera The Magic Flute, Barth later recalled, "They went right through me and into me, I don't know how, and I thought, 'That's it!' " From that day forward, Barth had a lifelong love affair with Mozart.

As he matured, his writing interests enlarged to include not only history but also poetry—though his poetry was inspired by his extensive reading in the history of warfare. He also wrote some plays, inspired by, among others, Friedrich Schiller's *William Tell*, about the great Swiss hero. He wrote his first play at age ten, *Prince Egan*, a play in five acts. This was followed by others, including tragedies, and one on the arrogance of the Berne aristocrats! Freedom played a key role in his plays, as did poetry and military history.

When in his fifteenth and sixteenth years he attended confirmation classes, he found himself surprised at his fascination with the content. The teachers spent a lot of time defending the rationality of Christian faith—something Barth would later repudiate as a waste of time—but he said the classes brought him "close to the problem of religion." He was so taken that, by the end, just before his confirmation and two months before his sixteenth birthday, he resolved to become a theologian.

He didn't realize at the time the unhappy direction theology had taken in the nineteenth century, nor the desperate need to engage it with all the firepower a theologian could muster. Barth's martial character did not serve him well as a boy, but it became indispensable for the battle he would fight as a mature theologian. He would grow from a terrible child into an *enfant terrible*—a man whose unconventional theology (for the times) would embarrass his liberal mentors and change the course of church history.

To understand what was at stake in the theological war that would erupt in the early twentieth century, we need to understand the history and nature of the theology that dominated the nineteenth.

CHAPTER 3

The Liberal Juggernaut

> *The 19th century theologians focused their attention on one particular point . . . : man's supposedly innate and essential capacity to "sense and taste the infinite."*
>
> —Karl Barth, "Evangelical Theology in the 19th Century"

It's not much of an exaggeration to call nineteenth-century liberalism a juggernaut, a "massive inexorable force [or] movement . . . that crushes whatever is in its path."[1] While Pietism and Reformed and Lutheran orthodoxy had their champions, the tenor and tone in the academy and church in Europe, and increasingly in America, was that of liberalism. This was the theology into which Barth was baptized and nurtured as he matured theologically. One cannot understand Barth and what his eventual theology and life were about without understanding what he eventually rebelled against. Thus we need to take some time here to outline liberalism's major themes and players, even if we must refrain from pursuing some of the finer nuances of their thinking.

The Rise of Reason

The liberal inclination has been a part of the church's life from the beginning, but it blossomed into full flower during the Enlightenment in the 1600s and 1700s. "The Enlightenment" is a catch-all term for developments in a number of fields—literature, art, science, and theology—that constituted a basic shift in perspective from the Middle Ages. There are many ways to discuss this shift, and good arguments can be made that it wasn't so much a break as a development. That being said, there were a few distinctives that ushered in a new era of intellectual history, beginning with René Descartes (1596–1650).

Descartes was anxious to find an assured, irrefutable basis upon which he could found a philosophy. He thought belief in a God whom we cannot see or touch, or directly and irrefutably experience, was not a firm foundation. As he looked for the foundation, he ended up looking to himself. He argued that the fact of his own existence was the only self-evident truth, the only truth that didn't need to be "proved." This was something he said we just know to be true. Only from this beginning point, he argued, could one construct a reliable philosophy and build on knowledge. He summarized this radically new way of approaching truth like this: "I think, therefore I am."

This shift in assumptions was profound and pervasive. It ended up affecting every field of human endeavor. It shifted the focus from God and his revelation to human beings, their history, their thinking, and their activity. This approach required another shift in thinking, equally profound: a much more optimistic view of human capability.

Descartes, for example, had to assume that his perception of himself and his experience was, in fact, not corrupted by original sin, that it was accurate enough to use as a foundation upon which to build a philosophy. Enlightenment theologians were not naïve. They still recognized that human beings were relatively ignorant and morally suspect. But, in the end, they believed that humanity was not so much in need of divine revelation—understood as truth that comes from the outside, necessary before one can make any intellectual progress—as in need of enlightenment, that is, insights discerned by reflecting on human beings and this world. Revelation, especially as it comes to us in the Bible, was still important for many theologians, but more and more because it offered insights and religious truths that completed and filled out a knowledge grounded in human perceptions and abilities.

In the end, Enlightenment thinkers determined truth not by revelation but by human reason and experience. While today many critique the straitjacket of Enlightenment thinking, in its day it was a liberating moment. Leading thinkers believed the medieval church had become oppressive, severely restricting the work of scientists, philosophers, and theologians to explore God's creation.

In fact, this is a caricature, as historians have shown; the church was in many ways the champion of academic exploration. James Hannam, in summarizing his *The Genesis of Science: How the Christian Middle Ages Launched the Scientific Revolution*, says that science "was seen as an essential area of study in its own right and for moving onto higher subjects. It was an independent field, separated from theology, which enjoyed a good deal of intellectual freedom as long as it was restricted to the natural world."[2] It was a topic that engaged the best minds of the era, such as those of Albert the Great and Thomas Aquinas. So, "in general, there was religious support for natural science by the late Middle Ages and a recognition that it was an important element of learning."[3]

But there were enough restrictions that intellectuals decided to push back. In the area of theology, for instance, Martin Luther and John Calvin challenged medieval theology and church practice. Again, it's not as if the medieval church had repressed all talk of grace and faith or completely abandoned the Bible. How else would a Luther or a Calvin have "discovered" grace and Scripture if these ideas hadn't been a part of the fabric of medieval faith? Still, theology had moved so far in one direction that, to Luther and Calvin and others, reforms were needed.

Overall, the Enlightenment felt like a refreshing breeze in a stale intellectual room. Enlightenment thinkers helped us see afresh that, despite our intellectual blindness and moral corruption, human beings remain capable of extraordinary things. The Enlightenment was a constellation of ideas, as Barth would later argue, that had unshakable faith in the power of human reason and will.

The Blossoming of Liberal Theology

But some problems immediately presented themselves to theologians. Many Enlightenment assumptions drove a wedge between reason and religion and created a gap that seemed unbridgeable.

No one drove this wedge deeper than Immanuel Kant (1724–1804), whose *The Critique of Pure Reason* (1781) became the classic Enlightenment text. In this and other works, Kant split human knowledge as scientists eventually split the atom, with equally devastating consequences for theology. Kant argued that there is a reality we can know by reason—that is, by evaluating human experience and knowledge. And then there are things that are impossible for reason to grasp—ultimate reality, like God and his attributes. These ultimate realities are a matter of intuition or a product of one's moral sensibilities. *Real* knowledge is scientific, a knowledge that can be tested by the dictates of reason. The other type of knowledge is, in the end, nothing but personal opinion.

So Kant's declaration in one famous essay of 1796 is a logical next step: We need to do away with all appeals to external authority, like the church and the Bible. We need to start thinking for ourselves, that is, let reason and reason alone be our guide. It is the only solid foundation for knowledge about ourselves and the world.

As a result, many believed that, to be faithful to the Enlightenment's insights, one had to abandon Christianity, with its deep pessimism about human nature. To be guided by reason, one had to abandon revelation. To be scientific meant forsaking religion. On the other hand, for many theologians, being faithful to the Christian tradition meant that one had to reject reason and the optimism about human ability. Many did, in fact, choose one or the other. But Friedrich Schleiermacher wasn't one of them. He believed he saw a way to combine the two, and it is his theological attempt to hold the Enlightenment and Christianity together that created what is known today as liberal theology.

Schleiermacher (1768–1834) seemed to be born to make this attempt. His parents were devout Christians who had experienced a warm, personal renewal of faith thanks to the Moravian Brethren, a branch of Pietism. Christianity, the Moravians taught, was not something one believed as much as something one felt and lived. Faith was cultivated through Bible study, preaching, and prayer and then sealed with active service to others. The Moravians also emphasized the need for Christians to develop a strong sense of community among themselves. While tending to be theologically orthodox, they put the emphasis on spiritual experience and practice.

Schleiermacher got a good taste of Pietism when he was sent to a Moravian boarding school at age fifteen. There he experienced both serious conversation and a growing interest in the intellectual life. Despite his religious experience, his curious mind was not satisfied with Moravian theology. In a series of anguished letters to his father, he revealed doubts about the most fundamental of matters:

> Alas! dearest father, if you believe that without this faith no one can attain to salvation in the next world, nor to tranquility in this—and such, I know, is your belief—oh! then pray to God to grant it to me, for to me it is now lost. I cannot believe that he who called himself the Son of Man was the true, eternal God; I cannot believe that his death was a vicarious atonement.[4]

As he continued his studies at the University of Halle, where rationalism reigned, he soon despaired of rationality as the sole basis of faith. From his studies and thinking emerged a book that would alter the course of European theology. In 1799, at the dawn of a new century, Schleiermacher published *On Religion: Speeches to Its Cultured Despisers.* In this book, he argued that those skeptics who had rejected Christian faith had failed to grasp the real nature of Christianity, which must be understood as a *religion.*

This may seem obvious, but Schleiermacher meant something particular. Religion, he argued, was not primarily about doctrine or ethics. In fact, he could be rather dismissive of those who thought such: "Belief must be something different from a mixture of opinions about God and the world, and of precepts for one life or for two. Piety cannot be an instinct craving for a mess of metaphysical and ethical crumbs."[5]

Instead, he argued that religion was first and foremost an internal experience, a spiritual disposition. He was not against knowledge or reason—in fact, he was trying in his own way to argue rationally for religion. But religion constituted a different kind of knowledge, a heart knowledge. Religion was feeling, having an *experience* of God and being aware of the divine in all of life. One can see clearly his dependence on Pietism in all this.

And, like the Pietists, he didn't reject thinking and doing, but he cast them in a new light, thus turning the intellectual tables on Enlightenment skeptics. A truly enlightened person could not be scientific if that person failed to recognize the reality of this type of knowledge—for it is clear that many experience it. At the same time, one could not be fully moral if one deprived oneself of the strength and motivation that religion supplies.

Schleiermacher could not have timed things more perfectly, because many people were already questioning the Enlightenment's unquestioned exaltation of reason. That countermovement is now called Romanticism. While the word "romantic" has a narrow meaning today, the overtones of that word still get at the core idea of the movement: human emotion and experience counted for something. Schleiermacher managed to combine the Enlightenment emphasis on reason with Romanticism's emphasis on experience.

Schleiermacher's mature theology was expressed in his *The Christian Faith*, one of the most influential works in Christian history. Here and elsewhere we find his assumption that "the essence of the religious emotions consists in the feeling of an absolute dependence."[6] This feeling is a universal experience, he argued, and thus it became a starting point for him. "I feel, therefore I am" is more or less the idea here. Again, this is similar to Descartes in that his theology is grounded on human experience rather than divine revelation.

Schleiermacher argued that Christians experience this reality through the person of Jesus. While Jesus was not divine in Schleiermacher's view, he was a man who had a perfect consciousness of God, unmarred by sin. From there, Schleiermacher reinterpreted the full sweep of Christian theology, always circling back to the priority of religious experience.

As these things go, some theologians said Schleiermacher had so reshaped Christian faith as to make it unrecognizable. But many believed that he had hit on something fundamental and took up his views.

Liberal Developments

One key thinker who developed Schleiermacher's insights in a new but still fundamentally liberal direction was Albrecht Ritschl (1822–1889). Ritschl had serious concerns about the priority of feeling and religious experience. Instead, he looked for something more objective, and for Ritschl that was history. History was open to scholarly investigation; by studying history, one could discern God's revelation of himself, especially by looking at the moral and spiritual impact of key people and events.

The central person and event for Ritschl was Jesus Christ. Ritschl rejected abstract theological speculation about the person of Jesus—whether and how he was human and divine, for example. Instead, he focused on Jesus's moral impact on his followers. Because of this, he concluded not only that God exists but that God was unquestionably and unusually active in Jesus. History shows that Jesus preached about the coming of God's kingdom and that this message changed people and improved society. It was his moral influence, not an atoning death, that made Jesus the bearer of salvation.

For all their differences, Schleiermacher and Ritschl were of one mind about the source of theological knowledge: human experience. For Schleiermacher, it resided in feeling. For Ritschl, it resided in morality. This emphasis on human experience is one crucial characteristic of the liberalism that came to dominate the nineteenth century. As Barth later put it, "The 19th century theologians focused their attention on one particular point . . . : man's supposedly innate and essential capacity to 'sense and taste the infinite.' "[7]

Barth's Theological Mentors

As Barth entered the university, he very much wanted to be a man of his times. His father's conservative theology held no interest for him, so when it came time to choose a university he aimed for Marburg, a bastion of liberal thought. His father refused, fearing his son would turn out liberal, but finally they compromised, and after a few semesters at the University of Berne, Karl studied one semester at the University of Berlin.

What a semester it turned out to be. It was at the University of Berlin that Barth's early liberalism took root. This is where Schleiermacher had taught two generations earlier, and his presence still hung in the air. Berlin is also where Barth immersed himself in Kant, the guru of the Enlightenment split between reason and religion. And it was at Berlin that Barth imbibed the lectures of church historian Adolf von Harnack (1851–1930), whose thinking seemed to be the destination toward which liberalism had been heading all along.

Six years before Barth arrived at Berlin, Harnack had dazzled the university with lectures that became the book *What Is Christianity?* In this and other writings, Harnack outlined his liberalism. For example, Harnack made a distinction between the kernel and husk of faith; the husk was useless doctrine that had over the centuries prevented the church from being nourished by the kernel. The kernel, or essence of the faith, was summarized succinctly as "the fatherhood of God and the brotherhood of man." This was the core of Jesus's message, argued Harnack, the message that had been obscured by church dogma. The obscuring process had begun even in the New Testament, with the writings of Paul and John, he said. All in all, Harnack talked about a God who was immanent in all creation and accessible to all people, for every person had a natural capacity to know God. Overall, it was a very optimistic view of humankind and its potential for moral and social progress.

Barth's father sensed that things theological were going adrift for his son. Fritz believed nothing good could come from Karl's forays into liberalism, which clearly was a denial of all that Fritz stood for. He insisted that Karl spend some time at Tübingen, a bastion of conservatism. Karl pushed back hard, but eventually he relented out of respect for his father. As these things go, Tübingen had the exact opposite effect on the younger Barth to what his father intended. After a semester listening to conservative theology, he was more convinced than ever that it was bankrupt. His father, seeing the futility of the situation, relented and let Karl finish his education at Marburg.

If Barth was baptized into liberal theology at Berlin, he was confirmed in it at Marburg. This is where Barth soaked in the lectures of Wilhelm Herrmann (1846–1922). Herrmann was a leading liberal theologian of the day and a student of Ritschl—though he departed from Ritschl in significant ways. Herrmann, for example, did not believe that history could provide the ground for believing that Jesus Christ was the bearer of God's salvation. Neither could science or philosophy or biblical proofs or theological reasoning. Religion was not a matter of deductions but an experience of the individual. And this experience could not be proven or demonstrated but only believed. It was self-authenticating; it did not require validation from another discipline.

The fact is, Herrmann reasoned, that Christ lived as a man among human beings. Though he was the revelation of God, this was not obvious to many people in his day, nor could it be discerned by historical research. His life and teachings could be observed by all, but his inner life, his intimate communion with his heavenly Father, was hidden. And yet this relationship is what made Christ divine and what links Christ and the rest of humanity. The unique moral purity of Christ is what led to the transformation of Christ's first disciples. Each subsequent generation catches a glimpse of Jesus's inner life by seeing the effect it has on his followers. Thus the experience of Christians is the source of revelation. Each individual believer could emulate Christ and thus experience something of the same intimate reality he had with God. Christ was sinless, of course, and experienced that reality at a depth we can only approximate faintly.

So, in rejecting Ritschl's confidence in history and the ethics of the kingdom of God, Herrmann returned to the insights of Schleiermacher—the essence of religion is a matter of experiencing the divine within.

Barth was stricken with all this during his three semesters in Marburg, and he eagerly attended Herrmann's lectures. After he completed his studies and was ordained in November 1908, he began trying on the liberal theology with which he had been clothed in academia. It would take him ten years to see how ill-fitting this theology was for the new century.

CHAPTER 4

Conversion

We have found in the Bible a new world, God, God's sovereignty,
God's glory, God's incomprehensible love. Not the history of man
but the history of God! Not the virtues of men but the virtues of
him who hath called us out of darkness into his marvelous light!
—Karl Barth, *The Word of God and the Word of Man*

After a brief stint as an assistant to Professor Martin Rade at Marburg, which included editorial duties and writing for a liberal theology journal, *Christliche Welt* (Christian World), Barth landed a pastoral position in Geneva in September 1909. He became the assistant pastor of the Reformed Church with special responsibilities for the German-speaking congregation. Here he began to learn his trade as he engaged in sermon preparation, visitation, and other pastoral duties.

His early sermons reveal the extent to which he had imbibed the teaching of his liberal professors. They are punctuated with lines like "The greatest thing is what takes place in our hearts," and "To each man goes out the call to be true to himself, namely . . . to that model of the best that anyone can become." In one sermon he told the congregation, "Try to become valuable!"[1]

The young pastor also taught confirmation classes, and it was in one of those classes he met Nelly Hoffmann. She was the youngest of five sisters whose father died when she was a year old, so the girls were brought up by their mother. Barth found himself impressed by the talented musician, and in May 1911, before he left Geneva, he proposed. Nelly was seventeen when they were engaged and Barth twenty-four, and they were married two years later, after Barth was well into a new pastorate.

Village Pastor

Barth left Geneva for the new parish in Safenwil, arriving in July 1911. Safenwil was an agricultural and industrial village, with a population of nearly 1,600. Of these, nearly 1,500 were Protestants. Like much of the Western world at that time, the village was slowly modernizing, with electricity introduced by the end of 1913. But more importantly, the valley community was losing its agricultural base to industry, mostly textile factories and wool mills. This transformation created social tensions in Safenwil as it did elsewhere in Europe and America, and these tensions would significantly shape Barth's early pastoral years.

But first there was the business of pastoring a church, and here, even more than in Geneva, Barth became aware of what it meant to be a pastor, preacher, and teacher.

In his sermons, Barth addressed his congregation as "my friends" or "my dear people"—the liberal fashion of the day. We find him early on lauding Schleiermacher as the brilliant leader of a new reformation. Barth's prominent themes were those of "life" and "experience," terms used often at Marburg.

Another early theme was his honesty. This meant admitting in some sermons that he didn't fully grasp what he was trying to say. But slowly it also started to mean telling his congregation things they didn't want to hear. In one sermon, he said, "Dear friends, the truth is not against anyone. It is for everyone. Believe me, I love you all equally, just as God loves us all equally." But "my calling is to speak and to speak clearly. . . . If I wanted to be liked, I would keep quiet."

Already, we see signs of theological things to come. Certain themes began to emerge long before he was shocked into a new way of thinking. "The message of Good Friday has its force . . . quite regardless of what you or I may say about it," he said in one sermon. And in another: "Jesus does not disappear when fine religious feelings disappear." And even this: "There is only one kind of work for the kingdom of God, the work that God does himself."

But as Eberhard Busch, the later assistant of Barth, who has written extensively about his mentor, puts it: "Statements of this kind stand out in Barth's early sermons like erratic features in a landscape which otherwise has quite different characteristics."

Whether it was his style or content (it is hard to tell from this distance), Barth's preaching did not engage the congregation, and only a small group continued to attend the church. It was mostly empty on Sundays. Barth later said, "I and the people of Safenwil were always . . . looking at each other through a pane of glass." Barth later felt bad about what he inflicted on his little congregation, feeling he was a failure. When he returned in 1935 for a visit, fifteen years after he left, he said, "I can see now that I did not preach the gospel clearly enough to you during the time when I was your pastor."

Barth took confirmation preparation as seriously he did his sermons, writing the curriculum himself. He expected as much dedication from his students. When one boy asked if he might miss the last three classes to attend a course on pruning fruit trees, Barth asked in return whether the boy wanted to spend the day of his confirmation among the fruit trees!

Barth was a pastor who became involved in the life of his parishioners' community. He served as one of the school governors and even became chairman of the board. In this capacity, he succeeded, among other things, in introducing sports for girls. When World War I broke out in August 1914 and a number of men were called to guard the frontier, Barth helped farming families by haymaking for weeks on end. He even occasionally shouldered a rifle while taking a turn in the home guard.

Young Socialist

One of Barth's more controversial activities was his political work. In this pastorate, he later recalled, he was "touched for the first time by the real problems of real life." He soon found himself learning about "factory acts, safety laws, and trade unionism, and my attention was claimed by violent local and cantonal struggles on behalf of workers."[2]

Since he took sides with the workers against the owners, many of whom were members of his congregation, Barth joined the Social Democratic Party. He read deeply in socialist and Marxist theory, and he was so convinced by it that he said at one point, "Real socialism is real Christianity in our time."[3] He taught classes to workers, trying to help them understand their situation from a socialist point of view. Barth discovered that this may have not been much of an evangelistic strategy—the Safenwil workers didn't necessarily start coming to church as a result—but the workers clearly liked Barth and began calling him "comrade pastor," while others called him "the red pastor of Safenwil."

His involvement with socialism—with its searing critique of the church for its comfortable relationship with the existing order—began to erode his confidence in the bourgeois religious ethos of liberalism in which he had been nurtured. So did the deep-seated angst about German culture that increasingly hung in the air. Many intellectuals considered the culture decadent and banal, only propped up by propaganda and lies. Many began to battle what poet Ernst Blass described as "the soullessness, the deadness, laziness, and meanness of the philistine world."[4]

Despite the appeal of these intellectual currents, Barth remained a member in good standing of the theological establishment and one of its ardent apologists. A catalyst was needed to bring the restlessness of the times to life in him. The catalyst that revolutionized the young socialist came, as these things often do, unexpectedly.

Shaking of the Foundations

Three years into this very active, challenging, and happy pastorate came news that Germany had declared war on Russia. The August 1, 1914, announcement was followed on August 3 by a declaration of war against France, and on August 4 with a British declaration of war against Germany. At the time, nations warring against nations was not unusual, as the history of Europe was replete with military conflict. This alone may have saddened but would not have shocked the young Barth.

What startled Barth was this: upon the declaration of war, ninety-three German intellectuals issued a manifesto supporting the military policy of Kaiser Wilhelm II and Chancellor Bethmann-Hollweg. As Barth noted, "To my dismay, among the signatories, I discovered the names of almost all my German teachers." This included Adolf von Harnack, Martin Rade, and Wilhelm Herrmann. Christianity, he later wrote, had been transformed "into 42 centimeter cannons."

It wasn't just that Barth thought the war unjustified. What disturbed him was the way these theologians, especially his mentor Herrmann, justified the war. He immediately dashed off a letter to Herrmann:

> We learned to acknowledge "experience" as the constitutive principle of knowing and doing in the domain of religion. In your school, it became clear to us what it means to "experience" God in Jesus. Now, however . . . an "experience" which is completely new to us is held out to us by German Christians, an allegedly religious war "experience"; the fact that the German

Christians "experience" their war as a holy war is supposed to bring us to silence, if not demand reverence from us.[5]

Barth scholar Bruce McCormack puts it this way: "If religious experience could give rise to such divergent and even contradictory conclusions, perhaps it could no longer be relied upon to provide an adequate ground and starting point for theology."[6]

As Barth pondered this news over the next few weeks, it became clearer and clearer that "the teaching of all my theological masters in Germany . . . seemed to have been hopelessly compromised by what I regarded as their failure in the face of the ideology of war." Their "ethical failure" indicated that "their exegetical and dogmatic presuppositions could not be in order." Thus "a whole world of exegesis, ethics, dogmatics, and preaching was shaken to the foundations, and with it, all the other writings of the German theologians."

He began to question not only his theology but also his calling in the church, that "religious workshop in which one is forged as a pastor." Once he lamented, "If only one could be something other than a pastor." He began looking for a way to break free of the niceness of religion that had been bolstered by a liberal ethic that merely reinforced the status quo. He was particularly annoyed at the "universal spoonful of tolerance which especially in our local church is proclaimed the supreme good."

He realized that part of the problem, and maybe the crux, was the way he had been taught to preach. Instead of being concerned with human "life" and "experience," he began to believe that preaching first and foremost had to be radically concerned with God. It was the first momentous step in in the journey toward a new theology.

Discovering a Strange New World

Over the next few years, Barth began to discover that the Bible was a book not so much about men and women but about God. In a lecture given during this time, "The Strange New World of the Bible," Barth said, "We have found in the Bible a new world, God, God's sovereignty, God's glory, God's incomprehensible love. Not the history of man but the history of God! Not the virtues of men but the virtues of him who hath called us out of darkness into his marvelous light! Not human standpoints but the standpoint of God!"[7]

As a result, he later said, he had to learn his theological ABC's all over again. He began reading the biblical books afresh, "more thoughtfully than before. And lo and behold, they began to speak to us—but not as we thought we must have heard them in the school of what was then 'modern theology.' "

The first-person plural here is not the royal "we." In Safenwil, Barth had become friends with fellow pastor Eduard Thurneysen (1888–1974), who pastored a church in Leutwil, a two-and-a-half-hour walk away. Every week, Barth would walk (and sometimes ride what he called his "trusty bicycle") "to talk and brood a lot."

They brooded about how to do ministry, about how to preach, about the church and its task in the world. "We did not know what great changes were in store at that very time," Barth later said. "We only knew that we had to look for decisive, compelling words, more substantial than those which we heard around us. And we knew that we could no longer do theology in the traditional style of the discipline."

At some point, Barth began to apply himself specifically to Paul's letter to the Romans. "I began to read it as though I had never read it before. I wrote down carefully what I discovered, point by point. . . . I read and read and wrote and wrote." Barth was thirty at the time, and he wrote out what he called his "copy book" to flesh out his new views. He did not intend it as a dissertation.

What Barth learned from his study of the Bible, and especially

Romans, was that, when it came to the Christian groups, trends, and movements of his time, "everything had always already been settled without God. God was always thought to be good enough to put the crowning touch to what men began of their own accord. The fear of the Lord did not stand objectively at the beginning of our wisdom."

He began to see not only a difference but a contradiction: "Our 'movements' then stand directly in the way of God's movement; our 'causes' hinder his cause; the richness of our 'life' hinders the tranquil growth of the divine life in the world. . . . The collapse of our cause must demonstrate for once that *God's* cause is exclusively *his own*."

When it came to the kingdom of God—a favorite theme of religious socialists—Barth realized that the Bible is talking about a radically transcendent idea. Some Christian socialists believed the kingdom of God is a slow but progressive political program that alleviates human suffering and ushers in human equality. Others saw it as a commitment to a radical way of life that only Christians could live out as they followed the Sermon on the Mount, a countercultural movement within the world. Barth started to believe that, no, the kingdom of God is not political or ethical progress within the old world, or even a rebellious, countercultural witness within it—but a whole new world. Humanity's religious and moral abilities cannot create anything new or fresh in history. This has to come from the outside. The kingdom of God is utterly God's work, from beginning to end, and cannot be realized until God decides to usher it in when Christ returns.

The Birth of a Revolutionary Manifesto

After filling two or three notebooks with such ruminations, he began coalescing his insights more systematically by writing a commentary on Paul's letter to the Romans. He began in July 1916 and had reached Romans 3 by September. He was so excited about the project that he worked himself to exhaustion. He had to ask the church council for a holiday to recover. During the next winter, he made only slow progress, reaching chapter 5 by March. Then he came to a complete halt for six months. He asked the church for a four-week study leave, which he was finally able to take after Easter in 1918. Gradually he was able to make progress, and on August 16, 1918, four years after his liberalism received its initial shock, he wrote in his diary, "Romans finished."

He then looked for a publisher. Three well-known Swiss publishers refused—he was an unknown pastor whose manuscript went completely against the grain of the day's theology. But finally one house agreed, but only because a friend of Barth supplied some necessary financial support. In other words, the original edition of Barth's *Romans* was more or less self-published. And then only one thousand copies were printed. Barth was correcting the proofs when World War I ended. It was in some ways the worst of times and the best of times to reground theology.

Barth wrote his commentary during the war's dénouement. The initial boosterism had turned into despair and even horror by 1916. In February 1917, the czar was overthrown in the Russian Revolution. The Spanish Flu had erupted in 1918 and lasted through August 1921, killing between 50 and 100 million worldwide, making it one of the deadliest natural disasters in human history. World War I mounted casualties upward of 37 million dead and wounded.

As the war dragged on, food shortages and inflation prompted protests in the German streets and also affected living conditions in Barth's Switzerland. Switzerland depended on foreign sources to supply 40 percent of its food and energy needs, but the outbreak of war cut those supplies short. Food and heating costs escalated. Cost of living doubled. Wages declined by 30 percent. Work days were lengthened without accompanying compensation. To pay for a number of services, including an army to protect its borders, a national tax was imposed, and still the national debt tripled between 1913 and 1925. Food rationing was instituted in 1917, and by June 1918, 18 percent of the population received government relief.[8]

It is impossible to believe that the collapse of confidence and optimism that imbued the late nineteenth century did not affect the writing of *Romans*. Many readers took his biblical commentary as mostly a social and philosophical commentary driven by the deep pessimism of the times. There is that, but Barth was trying to do much more. He was trying to articulate the power of the gospel in the midst of a social, political, and religious crisis. He was desperate to set the gospel on what he believed was its proper foundation. He did that in his first but especially his second edition of *Romans*.

CHAPTER 5

Romans—the Godness of God

*Our relation to God is ungodly. We suppose that we know what
we are saying when we say "God." We assign to him the highest
place in our world: and in so doing we place him fundamentally
on one line with ourselves and with things. . . . We confound time
and eternity.*

—Karl Barth, *The Epistle to the Romans*

In some ways, Barth's commentary hit the theological world with
a dull thud. His exegesis was rebuked by, among others, Adolf
Jülicher, the day's elder statesman of New Testament scholarship.
Reviewers compared him to the heretic Marcion. Rudolf Bultmann
thought his commentary an example of "enthusiastic revivalism."
His mentor Adolf von Harnack compared him with the radical revolutionary Thomas Münzer.[1]

Soon after publication, Barth met with Harnack and a friend of
Harnack. "The two gentlemen thought I would do better to keep my
view of God to myself and not make it an 'export article'!" Barth recalled. "Finally I was branded a Calvinist and intellectualist. Harnack's
parting shot was the prophecy that according to all the experiences of
church history I would found a sect and receive inspiration." What the
meeting suggested to Barth was that "The idol is tottering."[2]

It wasn't until after he gave a remarkable lecture at a socialist
conference at Tambach that Barth's ideas began to gain traction.

Only about one hundred were in attendance, but they were war-weary and eagerly looking for fresh ways to think about political and religious life. Barth's lecture, "The Christian in Society," repudiated the then-standard views of the Christian's political responsibilities, left and right: "The Kingdom of God does not first begin with our movements of protest. It is the revolution which is *before* all revolutions, as it is before the whole prevailing order of things." He rejected "secularizing Christ for the umpteenth time, e.g. today for the sake of democracy, or pacifism, or the youth movement, or something of the sort."[3]

The effect was electrifying, and word quickly spread that Barth had something unique to offer the times, so much so that Barth became something of a rock star among theology students in Germany. When Barth visited Erlangen, in the spring of 1921, a colleague noted:

> Seldom has a book had such a decisive impact upon theological students. . . . When at the end of the winter semester 1920/21, it became known that Barth was to spend a few hours at my house the next day, no less than twenty-eight people appeared without invitation—and this at a time when the majority of students had already departed.

Students who had "breathed the modern spirit" were seeking in Barth "something deeper," he said.[4]

What became irksome for Barth was not the pushback—he was a fighter, after all—but the misreading by theological allies. Emil Brunner thought in *Romans* Barth had taught that "part of our souls . . . is not imprisoned in the temporal and the finite, but has remained an undisturbed reservoir for the voice of God." Another reviewer thought Barth was affirming "the immanence of God in the human soul."[5] Not only had Barth not been sufficiently clear, but his theology during this period can only be compared to fast-frame photography. He quickly saw that the first edition needed significant revising to clarify what he was saying. He accomplished that revision at a feverish pace, composing the 521 pages in eleven months and sending the pages off to the publisher as he finished them.

"I shall never forget this hot summer," he wrote his friend Thurneysen. "I amble like a drunken man back and forth between desk, dinner table, and bed, traveling every kilometer with my eye already on the next one."[6]

In the preface, he noted his friend's silent partnership. Thurneysen

> has read the whole manuscript with approval, and has suggested many additions. Some of these additions penetrated deeper than my original comment, others were explanatory and added greater precision of expression. I have adopted these additions for the most part without alteration, and they remain a silent testimony to his self-effacement. So close has been our co-operation that I doubt whether even a specialist could detect where the one leaves off and the other begins.[7]

He completed the second edition toward the end of 1921, and it was published the following year. It was this edition that "landed like a bombshell on the playground of theologians." And this edition, the second, is the commentary that is best known and the most historically significant, whose themes continue to reverberate in our day.

Shock and Awe

The first thing that shocked the theological establishment was the form the commentary took. It was not a historical-critical, verse-by-verse examination of the historical and grammatical nature of the text. This was a theological commentary, an attempt to let Paul speak to the contemporary world. Barth took as his model the commentaries of John Calvin, who, Barth said, "first establishes what stands in the text, sets himself to re-think the whole material and to wrestle with it, till the walls which separate the sixteenth century from the first become transparent! Paul speaks, and the man of the sixteenth century hears."[8]

Second, *what* Barth heard Paul saying also startled readers. Barth saw in Romans a complete refutation of the human-centered religion of his day. Describing "the characteristic features of our relation to God," he wrote:

> Our relation to God is ungodly. We suppose that we know what we are saying when we say "God." We assign to him the highest place in our world: and in so doing we place him fundamentally on one line with ourselves and with things. We assume that he needs something: and so we assume that we are able to arrange our relation to him as we arrange our other relationships. We press ourselves into proximity with him: and so, all unthinking, we make him nigh unto ourselves. We allow ourselves an ordinary communication with him, we permit ourselves to reckon with him as though this were not extraordinary behavior on our part. We dare to deck ourselves out as his companions, patrons, advisers, and commissioners. We confound time and eternity. . . .
>
> Secretly we are the masters in this relationship. We are not concerned with God, but with our own requirements, to which God must adjust himself. . . . Our well-regulated, pleasurable life longs for some hours of devotion, some prolongation into infinity. And so, when we set God upon the throne of the world, we mean by God ourselves. In "believing" on him, we justify, enjoy, and adore ourselves.[9]

Or as he later summarized the problem: "For this theology, to think of God meant to think in scarcely veiled fashion about man, more exactly, the religious, the Christian religious man. To speak of God meant to speak in an exalted tone, but once again and more than ever about this man—his revelation and wonders, his faith and his works."[10]

Instead, Barth discovered in Romans "that the theme of the Bible . . . certainly could not be man's religion and religious morality, nor his own sacred divinity. The Godness of God—that was the bedrock we came up against. . . . God's absolute unique existence, power and initiative, above all in his relationship to men."[11]

The Godness of God

Barth pushed this idea to its limit. He argued that God as God could not be conceived of; he is beyond this world, wholly other, remote, alien, hidden. He drove home, in the words of Kierkegaard, "the infinite, qualitative distinction" between time and eternity, between humankind and God. Barth was desperate to demolish any notion that there is some preexisting connection between God and humankind, some natural capacity in human beings that gives them access to knowledge of God.

> Those who do not know the unknown God have neither occasion nor possibility of lifting themselves up. So is it with those who know him; for they too are men; they too belong to the world of time. There is no human righteousness by which men can escape the wrath of God. . . . Every concrete and tangible thing belongs within the order of time. Everything which emerges in men and which owes its form and expansion to them is always and everywhere, and as such, ungodly and unclean.[12]

He relativizes even "negative theology":

> Even negation of this world and perception of the paradox of life; even submission to the judgment of God and waiting upon

him; even "brokenness"; even our behavior of the "biblical man"—if these proceed from the adoption of a point of view, of a method, of a system, or of a particular kind of behavior, by which men distinguish themselves from other men—are no more than the righteousness of men. And even faith, if it proceeds from anything but a void, is unbelief.[13]

In short, he was toppling the liberal pillars of experience, ethics, and history, showing that, when it comes to knowing God, we bring absolutely nothing to the table. Not even tried-and-true analogies can bridge the gap between us and the God who is beyond all analogies.

For example, we see power in nature, and we use that as a starting point to talk about God's unlimited power. God's power, we assume, must be like nature's power, only God's power is just much greater, greater to an infinite degree. This is how the discussion of God's attributes often begins. But the very category of power, like all human analogies, Barth said, is merely a human construct and therefore inadequate to talk about God. God is not just an extension to infinity of the idea of power. Our notions of power are utterly inadequate to grasp the nature of God's power, which is beyond human imagination. God in this respect is completely unknowable and distinct from creation.

In some respects, Barth highlighted themes that Eastern Orthodoxy has been wrestling with for centuries. Theologians such as Clement of Alexandria, Gregory of Nyssa, Pseudo-Dionysius the Areopagite, and Maximus the Confessor talked about God's transcendence by means of apophatic theology, which is an attempt to tell us what God is not like—God is not bound by space or time, for example. God cannot be known in himself, Gregory Palamas argued, but only in his energies. Such theologians say that it is not even proper to say that God exists, because to say he "exists" is to suggest that his reality shares something of the reality of everything else that exists. But God's being is so radically different from ours that the word "exists" cannot do justice to his existence. Thus we cannot say that God "exists."

Such ideas have also been explored by many Western theologians, such as Thomas Aquinas, who balanced apophatic theology with cataphatic theology, that is, a theology that asserts positive things about God. But for Barth none of this went far enough. God is not simply beyond existence; he's beyond all our ideas about his being beyond existence!

If this is true, then how do these two realities—God and humankind—ever touch, for does not the Bible teach that they do in fact touch? Yes, says Barth, but not how we typically imagine it. There's an engagement, but one initiated and completed by God. If we are to know God, he must make himself known. There is no innate human capacity or gift for religious insight, no natural contact point that humans exploit to work themselves up to a knowledge of God. An encounter with God is nothing less than miracle, something God does from beginning to end. It is the "impossible possibility of faith—a possibility whose source lies in God alone."[14]

The connection is revealed in the very fact that the connection is impossible, that the gap between God and humankind is indeed unbridgeable:

> Grace is the incomprehensible fact that God is well pleased with a man, and that a man can rejoice in God. Only when grace is recognized to be incomprehensible is it grace. . . . Grace is the gift of Christ, who exposes the gulf which separates God and man, and, by exposing it, bridges it.[15]

And later,

> Faith is awe in the presence of the divine incognito; it is the love of God that is aware of the qualitative distinction between God and man and God and the world; it is the affirmation of

resurrection as the turning-point of the world; and therefore it is the affirmation of the divine "No" in Christ, of the shattering halt in the presence of God. . . . The believer is the man who puts his trust in God, in God himself, and in God alone.[16]

Barth is keen to remind his readers of the complete freedom of God. God is not bound to this world in any way. He is its judge. He can withdraw his divine favor at will. He is not a natural part of the created order, who can be assumed to be there whenever and wherever we call upon him. We have no right to claim his presence, power, or love.

When God, at his discretion, does intersect the world, it is not in obvious ways. Barth compares it to a tangent touching a circle, yet without touching it, so that when the world, by God's grace, recognizes that touch, it sees it not as a confirmation and affirmation of its existence but as a sign that this existence is transcended. This is what happened in Jesus Christ, especially his resurrection, which in turn throws light on the crucifixion, revealing its meaning.

But even in these events, in which God is with humankind and united to human nature in the flesh, God remains distinct from creation for Barth. If he were not distinct, then everyone would recognize him for who he is. Instead, he veils himself in the humanity of Christ, remaining hidden, unknown to the world—until he chooses to reveal through faith who he is in Christ. Thus God's revelation of himself in Christ is a revelation of his incomprehensibility, in fact, "the most complete veiling of his incomprehensibility"! This is the "God, who is distinguishable qualitatively from men and from everything human, and must never be identified with anything which we name, or experience, or conceive, or worship, as God."[17]

Thus God is not the opiate of the people, not one who merely makes them comfortable in their current existence, who makes their lives bearable, but one who upsets them, confronts them with a "crisis." The crisis is in part God's judgment on the pretension of human beings, who think they have God figured out. The crisis is also the knowledge that the God whom human beings thought they had figured out is utterly elusive, that he is not only beyond this world but beyond the Beyond.

Barth's Romans is, in some ways, one long commentary on the commandment, "You shall have no other gods before me." As Barth puts it simply, "Men are men, and God is God."[18]

One way this works itself out is in how Barth interprets passages that we instinctively imagine are about us. Take, for instance, Paul's statement, "Therefore, since we are justified by faith, we have peace with God through our Lord Jesus Christ" (Rom. 5:1). The temptation is to think Paul is speaking of peace as a feeling, as relief from the guilt of sin, or as an easing of the sense of alienation from God, or as a sense of God's nearness. But to think of peace in these ways is to think about ourselves, about what's happening to us inwardly. Barth doesn't deny that something happens to us and that this might elicit feelings of peace. But he's much more interested in what this peace represents objectively:

Peace with God is the peace concluded between man and God. It is effected by a God-given transformation as man's whole disposition through which the proper relation between the Creator and the creature is re-established, and by means of which also the only true and proper love towards God is brought into being—the love which has its beginning in fear.

Unless we are righteous before God, we must be at enmity with him; and love which obscures the distance between God and man and which is not grounded upon fear—as for example, the "intimacy" of mysticism, or of the romantics, or of the disciples of Zinzendorf—is, in the end, directed towards the "No-God" of this world and brings men under the wrath of God, as his enemies. . . . Peace is the proper ordering of the relation between man as man and God as God.[19]

Thus, even the way we read Scripture has become a monument to idolatry, a vehicle for thinking about ourselves, and then about God, and then only as he helps us with our religiosity.

As some of these quotations already suggest, Barth's unrelenting emphasis on divine transcendence, on the Godness of God, while they attack idolatry, also point to good news: "God himself propounds the problem of God—and answers it. He sets all men of all ranks always under one threat and under one promise. . . . But it is precisely this sternness of the gospel of Christ which constitutes its tenderness and gentleness and its power unto liberty. In his utter strangeness, God wills to make himself known and can make himself known."[20]

Be that as it may, Barth in this commentary gives no immediate relief, and he takes the argument into the heart of idolatry—religion.

CHAPTER 6

Romans—the End of Religion

No human demeanor is more open to criticism, more doubtful, or more dangerous, than religious demeanor. No undertaking subjects men to so severe a judgment as the undertaking of religion.
—Karl Barth, *The Epistle to the Romans*

B arth believed that the most powerful idol was religion itself, especially Christian religion. It is the preeminent idol precisely because it does not seem like an idol at all but the way one is faithful to God! But religion becomes a substitute for God, a way to avoid God in fact. With its rituals, ethics, and teachings, it not only takes for granted who God is and what he wants but imagines that it can manipulate God's presence and favor, and even manufacture by good will and good works the future, that is, bring in the kingdom of God.

The one who grasps that God is God knows that it is the very success of religion that is the problem:

He sees the inadequacy of the church growing apace, not because of its weakness and lack of influence, not because it is out of touch with the world; but, on the contrary, because of the pluck and force of its wholly utilitarian and hedonistic illusions, because of its very great success, and because of the skill with which it trims its sails to the changing fashions of the world. He recognizes that, precisely when the church attains the goal of service rendered by men to men, the purpose of God has been obscured, and judgment knocks at the door.[1]

This success breeds a spiritual confidence that signals the presence of sin at its most diabolical:

> Whenever men suppose themselves conscious of the emotion of nearness to God, whenever they speak and write of divine things, whenever sermon-making and temple-building are thought of as an ultimate human occupation, whenever men are aware of divine appointment and of being entrusted with a divine mission, sin veritably abounds—unless the miracle of forgiveness accompanies such activity; unless, that is to say, the fear of the Lord maintains the distance by which God is separated from men.
>
> No human demeanor is more open to criticism, more doubtful, or more dangerous, than religious demeanor. No undertaking subjects men to so severe a judgment as the undertaking of religion. The whole rich abundance of the worship of God, from the grossest superstition to the most delicate spirituality, from naked rationalism to the most subtle mysticism of the metaphysician, is under suspicion both from above and from below. God treats it as arrogance, and men as illusion.[2]

This doesn't mean that secularism, or even what later is called "religionless Christianity," is the answer:

> If religion is nebulous and lacking in security, so also is everything which is exalted to oppose religion. . . . To destroy temples is not better than to build them. . . . So long as religious as well as anti-religious activities fail to draw attention to that which is beyond them, and so long as they attempt their own justification . . . they are assuredly mere illusion.[3]

Thus Barth argues that, precisely because of its failures and idolatry, we need to remain in the bosom of the church: "We must not, because we are fully aware of the eternal opposition between the gospel and the church, hold ourselves aloof from the church or break up its solidarity; but rather, participating in its responsibility and sharing the guilt of its inevitable failure, we should accept it and cling to it."[4]

The more the church is the church, he says, we must stand within it "miserable, hesitating, questioning, terrified." But we stand "within the church, and not outside as a spectator." Our possibility is the church's possibility. The same is true of our mutual impossibility! Both the church's embarrassment and its tribulation are ours. We stand under the same judgment and are subject to the same impossible possibility of grace.[5]

A View from the End

In using the phrase "the end of religion" in the title of this chapter, I mean to suggest two related themes in Barth's commentary. The first is noted above, that Barth's theology signals an end to religion as a means of salvation.

For Barth, though, the end—or goal of religion and life—has to do very much with the end of all things, which is a second theme. All through his commentary, Barth announces the radical divorce between time and eternity, between now and then, between this life and life in the kingdom: "A Christianity which is not eschatology completely and without remainder has absolutely nothing to do with Christ."[6]

In exegeting Paul's declaration that "hope that is seen is not hope" (Rom. 8:24), he says,

Direct communication from God is no divine communication. If Christianity be not altogether thoroughgoing eschatology, there remains in it no relationship whatever with Christ. . . . Redemption is invisible, inaccessible, and impossible, for it meets us only in hope. Do we desire something better than hope? Do we wish to be something more than men who hope? But to wait is the most profound truth of our normal, everyday life and work, quite apart from being Christians.

Every agricultural laborer, every mother, every truly active or truly suffering man knows the necessity of waiting. And we—we must wait, as though there were something lying beyond good and evil, joy and sorrow, life and death; as though in happiness and disappointment, in growth and decay, in the "Yes" and the "No" of our life in the world, we were expecting something. We must wait, as though there were a God whom, in victory and in defeat, in life and in death, we must serve with love and devotion. . . . Existentially we see what to us is invisible, and therefore we wait. Could we see nothing but the visible world, we should not wait.[7]

Again, take his discussion of the peace of God, and note how he understands it eschatologically:

Peace is the proper ordering of the relation between man as man and God as God. Consequently, it is far more than a "pleasurable sensation of happiness," a sensation which may or may not accompany the conclusion of peace. . . . In it no union of God and man is consummated, no dissolution of the line of death, no appropriation of the Fullness of God, or of his Salvation and final Redemption. The bitter conflict between flesh and spirit remains as intense as before; man remains man, and God is still God. Nor is the necessity of faith removed, for the tension of the paradox remains without even the slightest easement. Men are compelled to wait and wait; they are impelled to hope, and not to sight. By faith, however, their waiting is a waiting upon God alone.[8]

Dialectical Theology

As is evident in example after example, the reader is assaulted throughout the book with Barth's dialectical theology. In the dialectical method, the writer uses two apparently contradictory truths in order to gain insight into reality. Barth believed that a full grasp of truth cannot be had by walking a straight line, where one grasps one idea and, building on that, is ready and able to grasp the next idea.

For example, in learning about chemistry, one is customarily introduced first to atoms, then to molecules, and then to increasingly complex compounds. The simple leads to the complex. One learns about the element hydrogen (and its symbol, H) and then oxygen (O), and then one learns that when two parts of hydrogen combine with one part of oxygen, one now has something called water, or H_2O. One piece of knowledge builds on another.

In the realm of science and everyday life, this way of learning may be all well and good. But Barth believed it is useless in theology and preaching. Barth believed that the deepest truths can be talked about only dialectically, that is, when complementary truths—or, better, contradictory truths—are discussed together. The entire theological enterprise, all God talk, is finally an impossibility. Yet theologians are required to speak about that which is ultimately unknowable. It is a vocation where reason is demanded and yet where reason is shown its utter inadequacy. Barth put it this way when he was a pastor: "As ministers we ought to speak of God. We are human, however, and so cannot speak of God. We ought therefore to recognize both our obligation and our inability and by the very recognition give God the glory."[9]

And in his commentary on Romans, he engages in dialectical thinking from start to finish: "Only when grace is recognized as incomprehensible is it grace." And: "Faith is awe in the presence of the divine incognito; it is the love of God that is aware of the qualitative distinction between God and man and God and the world." And: "In his utter strangeness God wills to make himself known."[10]

Given our usual approach to truth, we naturally balk at such statements. If grace is *incomprehensible*, how can it be *recognized*? And if there is a qualitative distinction between God and us, if God is "*utterly* strange," how can we possibly know about him, let alone have faith in him? And yet Barth replies that we "must be satisfied to live with this contradiction and not attempt to escape it."[11]

Most of us do not like living with contradictions, theological or otherwise. Psychologists call this cognitive dissonance, that uncomfortable feeling caused by holding conflicting ideas simultaneously. People have a powerful desire to reduce dissonance, and they will change attitudes, beliefs, and actions to relieve themselves of dissonance.

The classic example of cognitive dissonance comes from one of Aesop's fables, "The Fox and the Grapes." In the story, a fox sees some high-hanging grapes and desires them. But when he fails to think of a way to reach them, he concludes that the grapes are probably not worth eating; he reasons that they may not be ripe, or they may be sour.

In reading Barth, especially his paradoxical statements, one sees flashes of theological brilliance that entice us to learn more. We want to resolve the tension Barth sets up. When we find it impossible to reach this high-hanging fruit—the resolution that relieves the tension—we conclude that Barth is a sloppy thinker or that his theology is not worth consuming.

When it comes to theology, Barth believed that resolving, or resolving too quickly, the inherent tensions of faith is a crucial mistake, if an understandable one:

> The picture of a world without paradox and without eternity, of knowing without the background of not-knowing, of a religion without the unknown God, of a view of life without the memory of the "No" by which we are encountered, has much

to be said in its favor. It evokes confidence, for it is simple
and straightforward and uncramped; it provides considerable
security and has few ragged edges; it corresponds, generally
speaking, with what is required by the practical experiences of
life; its standards and general principles are conveniently vague
and flexible; and it possesses, moreover, a liberal prospect of
vast future possibilities.[12]

But for Barth, "The Gospel is not a truth among other truths.
Rather, it sets a question mark against all truths."[13] The gospel
doesn't build on itself, moving ever upward, step by logical step,
to some grand conclusion. Instead, it arrives at truth by shining a
bright light on the paradoxes and contradictions of our faith:

All "law," all human being and having and doing, the whole
course of this world and its inevitability, are a sign-post, a para-
ble, a possibility, an expectation. For this reason they are always
deprivation and dissatisfaction, a void and a longing. But once
this is recognized there appears above them all the faithfulness
of God, who forgives by condemning, gives life by killing, and
utters his "Yes" when nothing but his "No" is audible. In Jesus
God is known as the unknown God.[14]

Some tensions in the gospel are resolved in favor of the Yes
of God, but we nonetheless have to explore the No to grasp what
in fact has happened in the Yes. This is essentially the nature of
Barth's dialectic regarding Adam and Christ, the old world and the
new world, judgment and grace: Christ is the new Adam, the new
world has overcome the old (albeit eschatologically), and grace has
won out over judgment.

But other tensions remain, tensions that Barth explores with
vigor and power, and which give his commentary its characteristic features. There is, for example, as noted above, the dialectic
between time and eternity, between God and humankind. This is

probably the most important dialectic in the commentary. And then there is the dialectic of veiling and unveiling, which is most important in terms of Barth's lasting theological importance. These tensions remain, and in *Romans*, Barth is saying woe to us if we forget that they do!

The Sound of Bells

Barth later regretted the extreme nature of his polemic in *Romans*. He mocked some of his themes—like "Direct talk of God is not talk of God" and "Redemption is invisible, inaccessible, impossible and comes to man as hope"—by saying, "Well roared, lion!" He recognized that many of his remarks were "rash" but added, "I still think that I was ten times more right than those against whom my remarks were directed at the time."[15]

As noted, this was the book that put Barth on the theological map. It was not just the forcefulness of his prose or his ideas. He recognized that the timing could not have been better. With the suffering induced by World War I and the senseless loss of life (the Battle of Verdun alone counted nearly a million casualties), the bourgeois and optimistic world of liberal theology was in tatters. The response to the book astonished Barth, and he compared it to the time when, as a boy, he had mistakenly grabbed a bell rope in a church tower he had been climbing. The sound of bells pealed forth all across the town. "He did it unwittingly," he wrote of himself, "and he has no intention of doing it again."

Barth was clearly pleased that his words reverberated across the theological landscape. And he recognized that he was probably too pleased. For the rest of his life, he was fond of mocking his fame. In his own printed copy of this edition of *Romans* he wrote this dedication: "Karl Barth, to his dear Karl Barth, 1922." Then he added this quotation from Martin Luther: "If you feel or imagine that you are right and suppose that your book, teaching, or writing is a great achievement . . . then, my dear man, feel your ears. . . . You will find that you have a splendid pair of big, long, shaggy ass's ears."[16]

In one way, such self-deprecating remarks suggest Barth's humility. On the other hand, a man who is naturally humble need not mock himself like this. He did this sort of thing enough in his life to suggest that he wrestled with this demon all his days.

CHAPTER 7

Professor Barth

After much racking of my brains and astonishment, I have finally to acknowledge that orthodoxy is right on almost all points, and to hear myself saying things in lectures which neither as a student nor as a Safenwil pastor would I ever have dreamed could really be so.

—Karl Barth, in a letter to Eduard Thurneysen, 1924

The feverish writing of the second edition took place in the context of Barth's growing responsibilities, in the home and abroad. Matthias, his fourth child, was born to Nelly in April 1921, so this meant another mouth to feed. Fortunately, his star was rising, and he was being considered for prominent pulpits elsewhere in Switzerland.

He was also asked to consider becoming a professor of Reformed theology in the Lower Saxon town of Göttingen. The chair was being created by the Reformed Church of Saxony, with financial assistance from Presbyterians in the United States. Those creating the position insisted that Barth was the only one they would consider to represent Calvin at this Lutheran stronghold.

The offer was enticing but presented a few challenges. To begin with, Barth would be considered a second-class citizen at the university, because he did not have a doctorate, and he knew very little of Calvin, whose theology he was supposed to teach. In addi-

tion, he would be the only Reformed theologian on a faculty otherwise Lutheran. But when the formal offer came in May 1921, Barth
jumped at it, and by mid-October he and his family were on their
way to Göttingen.

"I am about to tread on some extremely slippery ice," wrote the
bold and brusque Barth to his friend Thurneysen. He even admitted
a certain dread: "I just can't imagine myself in the situation and
cannot think that I will be anything but a great failure."[1]

At the same time, he relished the opportunity. He recognized
that all he had done up to that point was to tear down. The new
situation suddenly required something more.

> Now it was no longer a question of attacking all kinds of errors
> and abuses. All at once we were on the front rank. We had to
> take on responsibilities which we had not known about while
> we were simply in opposition. Suddenly we had been given an
> opportunity to say what we really thought in theology, and to
> show the church our real intention and ability. . . . And yet we
> were far from being ready.[2]

As he wrestled with what exactly to say positively, he had before
his desk a painting he had picked up a few years earlier. It was a
reproduction of Matthias Grünewald's painting of the crucifixion,
as Barth put it, illuminating John the Baptist "with his hand pointing in an almost impossible way." John's hand points to Jesus on
the cross. "It is this hand which is in evidence in the Bible," Barth
said.[3] For the rest of his life, Barth worked with a copy of this
painting hanging above his desk. As Barth's positive contribution
slowly took shape, it conformed itself to this image, as a theology
where Jesus Christ stood at the center of things, with everything
and everyone pointing to him.

Confusion Within and Without

When Barth arrived in Germany in 1921, the country was in free fall. The terms of the Versailles Treaty ending the war devastated Germany. She was stripped of all her colonies; Alsace-Lorraine was returned to France; and West Prussia, Upper Silesia, and Posen were given to Poland. The victors demanded that Germany acknowledge sole responsibility for causing the war and compensate the Allies for losses and damages.

The amount of damages was set at the equivalent of $785 billion in today's US dollar. It was an amount well beyond Germany's ability to pay, even in installments. The government was forced to pay the first few installments by printing new marks, which only exacerbated the rising inflation.

In late 1922 Germany fell behind in payments, and in January 1923 France seized control of factories in the Ruhr, an area rich in raw materials for German industry. This only aggravated Germany's inability to pay reparations. Production took a hit, unemployment grew, and by August food riots were common. By the end of 1923 over 1,700 printing presses were churning out Reichsbank notes day and night. Marks were carried by armies of porters in straw crates. Often prices doubled in a few hours. A stampede ensued to buy goods and get rid of money before it devalued. By late 1923 it took 200 billion German marks to buy a loaf of bread. Many Germans found that their life's savings would not buy a postage stamp.[4]

It was not a peaceful or prosperous time to be a professor in Germany, especially a professor woefully unprepared to teach at the university level. Barth was responsible to teach about the Reformed confessions, doctrine, and church life, but when he took up his duties, he said, "I did not even possess the Reformed confessional writings, and had certainly never read them."[5] It had been ten years since he had read Calvin's *Institutes*, and even then he had done so through the lens of his mentor Wilhelm Herrmann. So he had to immediately and quickly immerse himself in Reformed theology and history.

The normally self-assured Barth wrestled with doubts. He wrote to his friend Thurneysen,

> Apart from the daily requirements, I have to build my own scholarly structure, achieve a "thorough mastery," as they say, in something. How does one do it? Will they ever be able to say that of me? Or shall I always be this wandering gypsy among all the honorable scholars by whom I am surrounded, one who has only a couple of leaky kettles to call his own and, to compensate, occasionally sets a house on fire.[6]

During one vacation he wrote, "I am much more conscious of my thorn in the flesh, my terrible theological ignorance, sharpened by my quite miserable memory. . . . Oh, if only someone would give me time, time, time to do everything right."[7]

He was both intimidated by and in awe of scholars such as Emanuel Hirsch and Erik Peterson, both his age yet already deeply learned. Peterson and Barth shared a similar theological outlook, but Hirsch was an ardent nationalist whose theological views Barth could hardly stomach. Hirsch would later become a member of the Nazi party and eventually adviser to Reichsbishop Ludwig Müller, the Lutheran bishop who became a minion for Hitler.

Senior theologian Carl Stange, an unrepentant liberal, invited Barth to participate in a bi-weekly theological discussion group, which included Hirsch. The initial cordiality broke down as Barth's popularity grew, because soon students were skipping Stange's lectures to attend Barth's. This did not sit well with Stange, especially since he scorned Reformed theology, once calling the Reformed Church in Hanover a millennial sect.[8]

In addition to academic jealousies, the political climate grew hotter. In June of 1922, after Walther Rathenau, a Jewish Reich-minister for Foreign Affairs, was assassinated by a right-wing, anti-Semitic extremist, Barth was invited with other scholars to the home of Walter Bauer, the famous New Testament professor. Most of the group condoned Rathenau's murder, causing Barth to lament again the comfortable, nationalistic liberalism of the times: "The German professors are really as bad as their reputation," he wrote. "What is one supposed to say when someone proclaims, with a bang of the fist on the table, that a Jew is always without a Fatherland and does not belong in a German government?"[9]

When the French occupied the Ruhr in January 1923, Barth said the move made his "blood boil with indignation."[10] It wasn't long before the effects of the economy reverberated in the classroom:

> Really, one asks oneself sometimes whether it might not be more sensible to toss all this theological rubbish into the corner . . . and transform oneself into a social worker. . . . One watches [the value of the mark] almost breathlessly. But in the meantime, people hunger and freeze notoriously in the thousands; tuberculosis and strange hunger diseases get the upper hand; students have to quit in the middle of the semester and take up another calling, because they do not have the means to go on. It is very bad.[11]

Budding Theologian

In spite of these formidable distractions, Barth's progress was remarkable. In his first few years, he taught courses on the theologies of Calvin, Zwingli, and Schleiermacher, the Reformed confessions, and church dogmatics—in addition to expositions of Ephesians, James, 1 Corinthians 15, 1 John, Philippians, Colossians, and the Sermon on the Mount! In his first semester, he had fifteen students for the main lecture and fifty to sixty for his lecture on Ephesians. The next semester, the main lecture had almost tripled—and his popularity only grew.

The discovery of Calvin was the thing that most bowled him over. Calvin, he said, is "a waterfall, a primitive forest, a demonic power, something straight down from the Himalayas, absolutely Chinese, strange, mythological; I just don't have the organs, the suction cups, even to assimilate this phenomenon, let alone to describe it properly."[12]

Being taught by Calvin, he wrote Thurneysen, meant to enter into dialogue with him. Calvin, he said, was the real teacher, and Barth and his classes were students. Barth was enamored with both Calvin's theological insights and his clarity of thought. He believed that Calvin's concept of God's sovereignty did not, as some critics supposed, undermine ethics but actually strengthened them. Despite Barth's reputation as a pessimist about human ability to please God, he was nonetheless intrigued with the topic of Christian ethics and establishing a proper foundation for them. He felt Calvin's theology helped him do that.

It wasn't Barth's intention to start a movement, but he had. And his theological allies increasingly felt a need to establish an organ by which they could share their views with the world. In January of 1923, *Zwischen den Zeiten* (Between the Times), a bimonthly journal, was started. Among its contributors were men whose names would grow in influence in the coming decades, including Emil Brunner, Friedrich Gogarten, and Rudolf Bultmann. Paul Tillich also traveled in these circles, but he was less interested in theology as such and more in culture and philosophy. In later years, Barth would have significant disagreements with each of these men, but in the beginning they were allies in countering the reigning theology of the day.

Between January and March of 1923, Barth and Adolf von Harnack sparred with each other in the pages of Martin Rade's *Christliche Welt* (Christian World). Harnack began by describing "fifteen theses to the despisers of scientific theology." He didn't address Barth or his theology by name, but he hardly needed to, given the theological climate. Barth replied with "Fifteen Answers to Professor Adolf von Harnack," which led to more exchanges. Harnack continued to maintain that scientific theology required one to study the Christian religion according to the norms of Enlightenment rationality. Barth argued that theology could only be scientific (that is, talked about rationally) in light of its own criteria. By that he meant God's self-revelation. As he said in *Romans*, only God can tell us about God. Barth noted once more "the magnitude of the gap that divides us," a gap that not only highlighted a generational divide but increasingly came to signal the passing of an era.

Pre-Dogmatics

The most important work that emerged from Barth's Göttingen years was a book that was never published in his lifetime, the *Göttingen Dogmatics*. It was Barth's first foray into dogmatic theology, and, as such, it introduced themes that would mark his later writing.

> I shall never forget the spring vacation of 1924. I sat in my study in Göttingen, faced with the task of giving lectures on dogmatics for the first time. Not for a long time could anyone have been as plagued as I was at that time by the question, could I do it? . . . I saw myself, so to speak, without a teacher, alone in the wide open spaces.[13]

One thing he was sure of was the audience for his theology. Dogmatics was not primarily written for the academy, let alone for Schleiermacher's "cultured despisers." No, "Dogmatics is reflection on the Word of God as revelation, holy Scripture *and Christian preaching*. . . . Its primary object, therefore, is neither biblical theology nor church doctrine, nor faith, nor religious awareness, but Christian preaching as it is actually given."[14]

It was also a theology that should not take its cues from culture or philosophy or even humankind's predicament. It had to begin with God's self-revelation in Jesus Christ. That meant, by implication, that Barth had to begin with the Trinity, for he had to understand and explain the relationship of Jesus Christ to the God he was revealing, and the work of the Holy Spirit in the very act of revealing this God.

This was a remarkable first step, given the dogmatics of that day. The Trinity had more or less been marginalized in Protestantism. It had been relegated to myth in liberal Protestantism, more or less ignored in Pietism, and trapped in philosophical speculation in Protestant orthodoxy. For Barth, it wasn't an explanation one tacked on to one's theology, as a kind of addendum describing God in more detail after the basics were covered. No, the Trinity was the basics, said Barth, and one could not begin discussing theology without first discussing the Trinity. If human beings were to know anything true about God, it was God who had to reveal himself to us. And he had done so decidedly in Jesus Christ through the Holy Spirit.

When he started in this direction, Barth found (contrary to his native liberal instincts) that he was inevitably moved to affirm the deity of Christ, the Virgin Birth, and a host of orthodox doctrines he had formerly repudiated. "After much racking of my brains and astonishment, I have finally to acknowledge that orthodoxy is right on almost all points, and to hear myself saying things in lectures which neither as a student nor as a Safenwil pastor would I ever have dreamed could really be so.[15]

On his way to discovering orthodoxy, Barth had run across a classic collection of Reformed texts selected and edited by Heinrich Heppe. Barth described the writings as "Out of date, dusty, unattractive, almost like a table of logarithms, dreary to read, stiff and eccentric on almost every page I opened."[16] But he also found something else: material that would allow him to fashion a new theology along the lines of the greatest theologians of the past, such as Augustine, Thomas Aquinas, and Calvin. What Barth found in the Heppe volume was a theology that allowed him to do theology in a way that was both grounded in tradition and yet creative.

Meeting the Catholics

During his time at Göttingen, Barth traveled extensively, giving addresses and lectures to enraptured audiences. It was an exciting time for him. "How huge and varied Germany is!" he wrote. "And there am I like a commercial traveler with my little briefcase, going to and fro from express to local train, in waiting rooms and on platforms, with a pipe which rarely goes out."[17]

In October 1925, after four years at Göttingen, Barth accepted an invitation to become the professor of systematic theology and New Testament exegesis at the University of Münster. The university was not only more receptive to Reformed theology but also a place where Barth would receive theological stimulation from a previously unmet challenger.

If Göttingen was a bastion of Lutheranism, Münster was a Catholic enclave. For the first time, Barth had a chance to interact with Catholic theologians, and Barth discovered he had a lot more in common with them than he did with liberal Protestantism. Whereas liberalism had watered down the gospel beyond recognition, at least Catholics continued to engage the church's great theological themes with respect: "It has kept at least the claim to the knowledge of the substance [of the faith] and has guarded it. . . . The substance may perhaps be distorted, but it is not lost!"[18]

Not that Barth was ready to convert. While acknowledging, for example, that both Protestants and Catholics believe in the "one, holy, catholic, and apostolic church," he thought Catholicism tried to control the church's unity, holiness, catholicity, and apostleship through its teaching office and the church's authority. Barth believed the Catholic Church acted as if it was the master of grace through the ministry of priests and sacraments. For Barth, grace was dynamic—not something that could be assumed; neither was it a given. Faith is a free gift, something that is perpetually offered and requires a perpetual response. All in all, the Catholic view was too static for Barth.

The biggest problem for Barth was Catholicism's use of the "analogy of being" to do theology. This method assumes that there is something innate in the being of humankind that has an analogue, a likeness, to the being of God, a likeness that can tell us something true about God. For example, human beings are relational, and this can tell us something about God being relational. Barth, however, did not believe that any such analogy resided intrinsically in the human person, but could only be given as a free gift of God in faith. Thus even the idea that we are created in the "image and likeness" of God is not a general human truth from which we can then discern who God is and what he is like. What our image and likeness mean, how they do and do not point to God, is not a given but a gift, something that is revealed to us in Jesus Christ. Only in light of Christ can we begin to grasp any analogies that may exist between God and humanity, and that light comes only by the free act of God.

Despite these and other differences, Barth found in Catholicism a worthy sparring partner for the rest of his life. One of the greatest Catholic theologians of the twentieth century, Hans Urs von Balthasar, was deeply influenced by Barth. In 1951 he wrote what was for nearly half a century the definitive interpretation of Barth (The Theology of Karl Barth), only surpassed by the work of Princeton theologian Bruce McCormack in the late 1990s.

Controversial Assistant

While at Münster, Barth entered into another unexpected relationship. During the summer of 1928, Charlotte von Kirschbaum began helping him with his research, expanding his card index. He had known her for years, and Barth had actually helped her with an "advanced examination" at college. In October, she returned with him to Münster, and for the rest of his active theological life she was his assistant. They shared not only deep mutual understanding and trust but also an untiring capacity for long hours of work. She helped as a partner, engaging and critiquing his work, and enjoyed extended breaks from work with him.

Whatever the exact nature of their relationship (about which there is much speculation), the relationship put a tremendous strain on his wife, Nelly, especially when "Lollo" moved into the Barth household to help him manage his workload. It was trying not only for the adults involved but for the children as well. The result was that everyone in the household "bore a burden which caused them unspeakable suffering," writes Barth biographer Eberhard Busch. "Tensions arose which shook them to the core."[19]

Whether or not the relationship was ever physically consummated, it was clearly a case of emotional adultery. Barthian scholar George Hunsinger acknowledges that Barth was "in love" with Von Kirschbaum. He also tried to set this relationship in context: In his younger years, Barth had been in love with another woman but was forbidden to marry her. This first love had died in her twenties, but Barth never recovered fully from the breakup, regularly visiting her grave for years afterward. His marriage to Nelly was, in fact, an arranged marriage, and not a happy one; Barth seriously considered getting a divorce at one point. So, without excusing Barth, there are elements that prompt some sympathy.

Barth and some later Barthians have tried to justify this relationship on the grounds that Von Kirschbaum was indispensable to his work, stating that he simply would not have accomplished as much without her. But that is to assume no other assistant was available who could have done an equally worthwhile job.

All in all, the simple fact is that Barth's understandable emotional emptiness got the better of him. That he enjoyed having a female colleague with whom he could converse freely and fully about his work was no doubt a great joy and helped him immensely. But husbands of lesser stature have recognized that when such a relationship sabotages the very integrity of one's marriage and becomes a burden to one's family, it may suggest a duty to sacrifice one's desires for the sake of one's vows. That Barth failed to see this and act accordingly suggests that he was, as he often acknowledged, a sinner.

He is not the only Christian of note with a significant personal flaw who nonetheless communicated the truth and grace of God in extraordinary ways. To take but one example: The saintly Francis of Assisi, who has often been called "the second Christ," battled with spiritual pride to the end of his days. Be that as it may, we cannot understand Barth without recognizing that at every step of the way, from this point forward, Charlotte von Kirschbaum was at his side, as secretary, confidant, and colleague. Her contributions to his theology have only begun to be explored but are no doubt considerable.

Despite the decades of grief this caused the marriage, in later years Nelly and Karl seemed to have been reconciled over this matter, especially after Von Kirschbaum had to be committed to a nursing home because of Alzheimer's. Karl and Nelly together visited her every Sunday for years. In fact, after Karl passed away, Nelly continued the weekly visits to the woman who had given her so much heartache.

CHAPTER 8

Resistance

I was thoroughly wrong at the time in not perceiving danger in National Socialism.... Its ideas and methods and leading figures all seemed to me to be quite absurd.

—Karl Barth, 1962

In late 1929 Barth received an invitation to become chair of systematic theology on the Protestant faculty of the University of Bonn. He finished his duties at Münster, and in March 1930 he, his family, and Von Kirschbaum moved to Bonn. With this appointment, Barth's influence began to be felt even more widely.

The impact on the theological faculty was immediate: enrollment doubled and continued to grow, for a time up to some four hundred students. Barth's main lectures were held in a hall that held over three hundred students, and the room in which he lectured was nearly always filled to capacity. So popular were his seminars that he had to limit them to thirty students, with another thirty taking the course by audit. These students, in turn, went forth from Bonn carrying the theology of Barth to the uttermost parts of the earth.

One thing that surprised Barth was how little interest his Bonn students showed in nineteenth-century theology, the theology that had formed him and which he had so vigorously opposed. Considering the vehemence of his opposition to liberalism, his concern about his students reveals a more complex Barth:

I would be very pleased if they [the students] were . . . to show a little more love toward those who have gone before us, however alienated they feel from them. . . . We need openness toward particular figures with their individual characteristics in which they worked; much patience and a good sense of humor when we consider their limitations and weaknesses; a little grace in expressing even the most profound criticism; and finally (even in the worst cases) a certain tranquil delight that they were as they were.[1]

When it came to contemporary theological opponents, however, Barth remained relentless. In this case, "one faces people who can still be shaken, from whom one can expect further developments, whose arguments and counter-arguments call for some sort of reply."

During his years in Bonn, Barth had plenty of opponents, theological and political, whom he felt needed to be shaken. It was in Bonn that he began a lecture series that would, year by year, turn into his famous *Church Dogmatics* (to which we will turn in later chapters). It was also in Bonn that Barth's theology shaped the unique nature of the church's resistance to one of the great evils to arise in the twentieth century.

Political Turmoil

The day before Barth arrived to take up his teaching duties in Bonn, the cabinet of German Chancellor Hermann Müller had resigned, and three days later a new government was formed under Heinrich Brüning of the Catholic Center Party. It was the fifteenth government of the Weimar Republic (which replaced the empire in 1919) and, for all intents and purposes, the last.

This turnover signaled once more that the political and economic situation in Germany was in chaos. Unemployment had skyrocketed to 1.5 million since the recession of the winter of 1928–29. The October 1929 US stock market crash, whose effects reverberated all over the world, only made matters worse in Germany.

Taking advantage of a clause in the Weimar constitution, Brüning convinced the president, Paul von Hindenburg, to assume emergency powers, which gave him the right to enact policy by decree. Under Brüning's leadership, taxes were raised and the budget slashed. When the Reichstag (the German name for parliament and the building in which it met) rejected his policies, Brüning dissolved it and called for a new election. During the election, communists and the National Socialists played on the economic unrest and fomented violence. But when the dust cleared in September, the National Socialists had gained 18.3 percent of the vote, five times the number they had achieved in the previous election. They were now the second largest party.

Brüning was unable to form a pro-republican ruling majority, and his government became dysfunctional. Employment rose to 5.6 million by February 1931, and presidential decree after presidential decree proved ineffectual to stem the tide. The National Socialists exploited the national malaise by organizing public demonstrations and paramilitary violence.

Barth had more or less ignored politics since 1921, but with the election of September 1930 and the sudden success of the National Socialists, Barth began to rethink his political passivity. He later regretted his tardiness, saying, "I was thoroughly wrong at the time in not perceiving danger in National Socialism. . . . Its ideas and methods and leading figures all seemed to me to be quite absurd. I thought that the German people were simply too sensible to fall prey to that possibility."[2]

But by early 1931, "when rightwing terror was gaining the upper hand, I thought it was right to make it clear with whom I would like to be imprisoned and hanged." What that meant was that Barth joined the Social Democratic Party. He wasn't affirming socialism as much as identifying with a party he felt was most aware of the "requirements of a healthy politics." He also wrote articles that implicitly or explicitly attacked the National Socialists. Late that year, for example, he argued that fascism is a religion. It had "deeply-rooted, dogmatic ideas about one thing, national reality." It appealed to "foundations which are not foundations at all." It was exalting "sheer power." And it was a religion from which Christian faith could only expect opposition.[3]

German "Christians"

Most Christians in Germany, however, could not fathom what Barth was talking about. Most German Protestants were as bitter toward the Weimar Republic as were fascists and other conservatives. They lamented the shameful loss of the World War, which precipitated the demise of the empire and the collapse of the princely houses. They were scandalized by the rising power of socialists and the influence of the Roman Catholic Center Party.

They were especially grieved when the close ties between church and state were cut, financial arrangements altered, and even some church schools threatened with closure. Many Protestants condemned these developments, blaming secularism and the collapse of moral values. In 1922, twenty-eight provincial Protestant churches organized themselves into a loose national federation of churches. They were able to apply some political pressure and win back some privileges, but it was still nothing like it had been in the glory days under Bismarck, when Protestantism and empire ruled side by side, and the prestige of Germany was at an all-time high. These Protestants felt like strangers in their own land.

The National Socialists (and their leader, Adolf Hitler) shared the bulk of these Protestant sentiments; so when they suddenly rose to power, many Protestants thought they had found a national savior. Hitler in fact hated Christianity and believed it incompatible with National Socialism. But German Protestants failed to notice this amid his promises of renewed prosperity, his resentment of the Versailles Treaty, and his vision of restored German glory. They resonated with his hatred of socialism and communism and his call for law and order, for discipline, and for greater public morality.

The Brüning government, in disarray, finally collapsed at the beginning of 1933, and Hitler was sworn in as chancellor on January 30. That day, Barth was in bed with the flu, but he later remembered his feelings upon hearing the news: "[I] immediately knew where I stood and what I could not do. . . . I saw my dear German people beginning to worship a false God."

A month later, the Reichstag burned to the ground. Arson was blamed on the Communists, who were said to be starting a coup. The destruction of the national symbol at the supposed hands of communists was more than enough reason for Hitler to declare another state of emergency. By means of what is called "The Enabling Act," he convinced the Reichstag to grant him plenary powers on March 24, making him virtual dictator.

Among Hitler's first acts was the banning of competing political parties, especially the communists, and arresting their members. After another election in early March, Hitler and his National Socialists were in virtual control of the government.

Hitler realized how deeply the Christian tradition ran in German veins, so despite his personal animus toward Christianity, he had no intention of alienating this group. In a speech on the day before the Enabling Act passed, Hitler reassured all the churches (though in this speech mostly Catholics were in view):

> The national Government sees in both Christian denominations the most important factor for the maintenance of our society. It will observe the agreements drawn up between the churches and the provinces; their rights will not be touched. . . . The Government will treat all other denominations with objective and impartial justice. . . . The national Government [sees]

in Christianity the unshakable foundation of the moral and
ethical life of our people.

At the same time, Hitler hinted at what would be in store for
churches that resisted his political program:

The Government, however, hopes and expects that the task of
national and ethical renewal of our people, which it has set
itself, will receive the same respect by the other side.... It
cannot, however, tolerate allowing membership of a certain
denomination or of a certain race being used as a release from
all common legal obligations, or as a blank check for unpun-
ishable behavior, or for the toleration of crimes.[4]

Hitler and the Churches

At the time, only a handful of Christians, represented by men such
as Karl Barth and Dietrich Bonhoeffer, understood the grim import
of these words.

Barth saw that the German Protestant church was woefully
unprepared for this moment, "even incapable of recognizing the
National Socialist state as . . . opposition." The Protestant church
had been shaped by "other less ostentatious and aggressive alien
pressure to such a degree that it simply could not repudiate . . . the
crude assumption that the church . . . could be assimilated into
the National Socialist State." Over the next few months, Barth was
especially grieved to see that many friends and theological allies
not only were enthusiastic about the National Socialists but also
sought ways for the church to cooperate with its political agenda.

Still, Barth was no political revolutionary. He urged his students, in fact, to keep on working as normally as possible in this
situation. Continue to read and study and discuss theology, he said.
That was his and their vocation, and when it came time to address

the political situation they must do it theologically. This meant for Barth that Christians should abandon finally and completely any notion of natural theology, a theology that posits an inherent point of contact between God and humankind, the idea that one could discern God in the fabric of the created order and/or history—just the sort of thing German Christians were doing in spades.

In the course of the next few months, Hitler pacified the Catholics, who counted for 40 percent of the German population. Catholics found their ultimate source of human authority outside the borders of Germany, and for the feverishly nationalistic Nazis this was unacceptable. Yet Hitler could not simply ban Catholicism or insist that Catholics ignore the pope. So in July his government worked out a concordat with the Roman Catholic Church, to the effect that the German government was to stay out of the affairs of the church, and the church would cease all its political activity. Formally, the agreement established the rights of the Catholic Church under the new regime, but Hitler used it as propaganda to suggest that the Catholic Church supported him. The Catholic Church did not see it that way at all: For the Catholic hierarchy, it was the only agreement possible under totalitarian circumstances. Any other agreement would likely have meant the end of the Catholic Church in Germany. (By 1937, however, Hitler had started harassing the church and arresting priests anyway.)

When Hitler turned his thoughts to the Protestant church, the situation looked dizzying. There were at least twenty-eight different church federations, and the national assembly of these churches had no real authority, let alone single figurehead. Hitler decided they needed a figurehead, a national bishop who would participate in the Ministry of Cults (religious affairs) at the national level.

The response of German Christians to this idea was immediate and enthusiastic, for they could clearly see what it signaled.

Through God's intercession, our beloved German Fatherland has experienced a mighty exaltation. In this turning point in history we hear, as faithful evangelical Christians, the call of God to a closing of ranks and a return, the call also for a single German Evangelical Church. . . . The Confessions are its unalterable basis. . . . A national bishop of the Lutheran confession stands at its head. . . . Christ comes again and brings an eternal completion in the majesty of His Kingdom.[5]

To be fair, not all Protestants agreed, but general euphoria was growing. Protestants once again had a significant role in national affairs. A strong, national, and unified church could be imagined. Added to this was growing economic optimism, the suppression of leftists, the possibility of restored national greatness—could all this be mere coincidence? Was it not a clear sign of God's hand at work? How could one avoid the conclusion that Adolf Hitler was God's chosen instrument in all this? Did not all this coincide with what was already happening in some quarters of the church?

Indeed it did. Already in 1932, before Hitler came to power, a number of Christians had joined forces to create a movement that championed the Nazi party's ideal of "positive Christianity." This was an attempt to meld Christianity with Nazi ideology. "Positive Christianity" rejected the traditional doctrines of sin and human depravity, as well as many of the classic Christian virtues, such as humility. The ethics of the Sermon on the Mount were said to be for life in heaven only. All church confessions were rejected in favor of the doctrines of race and people, of blood and soil.

Instead of working for the far-off kingdom of heaven, the faithful were to march with the nation in bringing about a paradise here and now. Christ came to help Germans fulfill their historic role as a unique and supreme people. Did not nature show that there were superior and inferior races, and that God in his providence had raised up the superior races to lead humankind to its ultimate destiny? This would require struggle, of course, even war. But how else would the unequaled religion of Christianity and the greatest nation on earth ever reign supreme? This was what was required of the super race, the Herrenvolk, which in order to remain strong and pure had to reject Jews, blacks, and other non-Aryans. And at the head of this super race now stood Hitler, manifestly God's chosen instrument for these times.

Not all German Christians went so far. Some banded together merely to have a voice in government once again. But over the coming months and years, as the National Socialists enjoyed success after success, more and more Christians became enamored with "positive Christianity." History seemed to confirm its beliefs.

German Christians increasingly held key positions in every provincial church governing body and were openly supported by Nazi party members and officials, some of whom in turn became church members. It was very much the patriotic thing to do, the church and state working hand-in-hand to strengthen German morals. Storm troopers and Hitler youth often came to church in all their regalia, and military bands were often invited to play in churches. How inspiring it must have been to see strong, young, male leadership in uniform sitting proudly in the front pews of the church. It surely signaled a bright future for church and country.

Early Resistance

Barth, of course, was aghast at such developments, and in classroom and traveling lectures he urged Germans to abandon "all and every kind of natural theology, and dare to trust only in the God who has revealed himself in Jesus Christ." The place to begin thinking about God's involvement in history is not in history, in what's happening around us, he said, but in the revelation of God in Jesus Christ. That revelation tells us that leaders who exalt themselves, who glorify power, who demonize Jews, who brutalize the opposition, and who seek to compromise the faith and unity of the church are not merely unjust but the antichrist.

In April 1933 the Law for the Reorganization of the Civil Service was passed, barring all Jews from civil service. Professors, who were hired and paid by the state, were civil servants and thus subject to the law. It was the means to marginalize not only Jews but all who were not anti-Semite. The law became the pretext to question the loyalty of a number of professors and to transfer or dismiss them from posts. The Social Democratic Party wrote its members suggesting that they resign from the party but hold their views privately. Paul Tillich was one professor who thought it good advice, and he wrote Barth encouraging him to resign his membership. Barth would have none of it. He wrote back, "Anyone who does not want me like this cannot have me at all."

Barth made more or less the same speech to Bernhard Rust, the Prussian Minister of Cultural Affairs. Given his convictions and continued membership in the Social Democratic Party, Barth asked Rust if he was going to be permitted to teach. Rust said yes, as long as Barth did not form cells in which to agitate politically. That gave Barth breathing room to teach at least through 1933.

Barth did not form cells, but he continued to think and act theologically about the events that were engulfing the church. In June, he played a decisive role in writing "Fourteen Düsseldorf Theses," the first public statement coming from a church body (in this case, the Reformed Church), warning of the present danger. The first thesis was identical to the first thesis of the Berne disputation of 1528: "The holy Christian Church, whose sole head is Christ, is born of the Word of God, keeps to it and does not harken to the voice of a stranger."

That same month, as Hitler granted increasing authority to Müller and the German Christians, Barth composed a pamphlet whose title is translated as *Theological Existence Today*, a blistering comment on unfolding events. The teaching of the German Christians was nothing less than heresy, he said. Church membership is not determined by blood or race. The church doesn't have to "serve men and so it does not have to serve the German people." Even in the Third Reich, the church must continue to proclaim the gospel.

The publisher of the pamphlet, Kaiser Verlag, worked day and night to publish and distribute it. Because of high demand, a second edition had to be printed within weeks. It was finally banned within the year, but not before some 37,000 copies had been published, and one copy sent to Adolf Hitler courtesy of Karl Barth.

At this time, Barth found it necessary also to distance himself from another Christian group, the moderate Young Reformation Movement. These Christians agreed with him that the church as church should not assimilate with the state or champion its political program. It should remain formally independent, eschewing political involvement. At the same time, as individuals they affirmed the direction the Nazis were taking the country, what Barth called a "joyful yes to the new German state." To Barth, this was a compromise that was really no compromise but only another form of capitulation.

Barth could only reiterate what he had said on other occasions: that the church can have no other gods than God, that the Bible was enough to guide the church, that the grace of Christ was enough not only to forgive sins but to shape the church's life.

In the meantime, the German Christians had gathered and adopted a new constitution, which became national law on July 14, 1933. Elections for various offices in the German Protestant church ensued, with candidates supported by German Christians, a group called Gospel and Church (essentially the Young Reformation Movement), and another called For the Freedom of the Gospel, which Barth helped start. In the end, though, it was a huge victory for the German Christians, and within months they had consolidated power in the Protestant church.

In early September of 1933 the Prussian Synod, the largest regional church, passed the Church Law concerning the Legal Status of Ministers and Church Officials, which included the infamous Aryan paragraph: non-Aryans and those married to such were now forbidden to be employed in the church. A few weeks later, Ludwig Müller, a man very much on board with Hitler's agenda, became

Reichsbishop of the Protestant church in Germany. With these and other steps, the power of German Christians seemed complete.

The first signs of collective resistance among Protestants was the formation of the Pastors Emergency League, set up by Pastor Martin Niemöller and other ministers. The League called on pastors to sign a four-point declaration that bound them to Scripture and the confessions and rejected the Aryan paragraph. Six thousand pastors immediately signed on, about one-third of all Protestant pastors. But, to be clear, this was a protest against state interference in the life of the church, not a general protest against Hitler's policies. There was still support for many of Hitler's policies. For example, when, a month later, Hitler ended Germany's membership in the League of Nations, the Pastors Emergency League congratulated the Führer.

It was incidents like this that made Barth despair. He wanted the church not to protect only its own interests but to speak truth in the face of the national evil. Even before the September events, Barth had refused to participate in the Reich church government at all. In the July elections he had actually won a seat in the local presbytery, but he would not take it because he believed the church had become utterly compromised. "All along the line, Christians and theologians have shown themselves to be a much weaker, more glutinous and more ambivalent group than we ever dreamt," he said.

Unfortunately, such dramatic acts and hard words alienated him from some of his close friends, so that he would complain, "Why must I be so isolated, even among those honest people with whom I would so like to agree and yet with whom I disagree so grievously?"

CHAPTER 9

Barmen

Jesus Christ, as he is attested for us in Holy Scripture, is the one Word of God which we have to hear and which we have to trust and obey in life and in death.

—Barmen Declaration, 1934

As these things go, the German Christians finally overstepped the bounds of decorum. It happened at a November 1933 gathering of German Christians in Berlin, where twenty thousand assembled in the Sports Palace. The meeting began with delegates booming out Luther's "A Mighty Fortress Is Our God." That was followed by fiery speeches and hard-line resolutions that went too far.

The church's doctrines and historic confessions were attacked. All Jewish elements in the church and its teaching needed to be discarded, the speakers said, and no Jews and blacks allowed in church. The Old Testament, a book riddled with the myths of the Jews, needed to be purged from Bibles. German Christians should no longer think of themselves as humble servants of a Jewish messiah, but as proud soldiers of a militant Christ. There should be no more talk of the crucified Christ, but only of King Christ and the Führer.

Dr. Reinhold Krause, a senior Nazi official, attacked Barth by name. As Krause pit the heroic Jesus against the Old Testament and lamented the Jewish element in the New, he scorned "dialectical theology from Paul to Karl Barth."[1]

The event exposed to a shocking degree how racist and compromised the German Christians had become. Afterward, even moderate Protestants who still supported the Nazis thought things had gone too far, and many deserted the German Christian movement. Opponents were shocked. Barth simply said, "Now we all have reason to be ashamed before God and his angels."

Even the Nazi leadership saw a public-relations disaster in the making. Instead of co-opting the church and making it complacent, they had aroused strong opposition within the church to both German Christians and the government. So the party distanced itself from the German Christians, as did Bishop Müller. And from this point forward, the German Christians as a movement lost steam—though the movement's views still captivated the hearts and minds of many German believers.

Bishop Müller continued to work in concert with the government, and at the end of December he startled the churches by signing an agreement whereby the 600,000 to 700,000 members of the Evangelical Youth Organization were now to become Hitler Youth. Many protested the move, but to no avail. Youth who refused to go along were treated as outcasts by classmates or disciplined by authorities.

Müller also announced what came to be called the "Muzzling Act," which forbade churches from using their services "for political affairs, in whatever form"—including criticizing the church government. This was Müller's response to pastors in the Emergency Pastors League who, after the Sports Palace debacle and the Hitler Youth agreement, had issued protests in pulpits throughout the land. But a council of Lutheran bishops endorsed Müller, marginalizing the protesters. Then punishments were meted out: some pastors were forced into retirement, others banished to remote rural parishes. In the end, the government pushback convinced two thousand pastors to withdraw from the Emergency Pastors League.

To Barmen

As the calendar turned to 1934, things looked increasingly bleak for any Christian who sought to resist the Nazi tsunami. Barth, however, was only warming up.

In these bleak months, Barth wrote to his friend Dietrich Bonhoeffer, who was in England, pastoring two German congregations. It was a self-imposed exile, one about which Bonhoeffer was conflicted. He wrote to Barth, whose seminars he had attended and whom he considered a theological mentor.

> I felt that [in Germany] I was incomprehensibly in radical opposition to all my friends, that my view of matters was taking me more and more into isolation. . . . I was afraid that I would go wrong out of obstinacy—and I saw no reason why I should see these things more correctly, better than so many able and good pastors—and so I thought that it was probably time to go into the wilderness for a while.[2]

Barth, who knew something of the loneliness of standing firm in the circumstances, would have none of it. He wrote back, telling Bonhoeffer that he should stop playing "either Elijah under the juniper or Jonah under the gourd" and should come back "on the next ship." Bonhoeffer eventually followed the advice, but not for many months. (Later Barth was tormented with the thought that his advice had ultimately sent Bonhoeffer to his death.)

At the end of January, Barth was invited to Berlin to attend an assembly of church leaders and theologians who were preparing for a visit of Adolf Hitler to the Protestant church and its two camps. Barth was asked to agree to a memorandum introduced by Tübingen theologian Karl Fezer. After Barth read it, he was horrified and said he regarded it as heretical. He told Fezer, "We have different beliefs, different spirits, and a different God."

Immediately tumult broke out in the room. Fezer turned pale, and someone shouted, "Can Barth be serious?" Some wanted to throw Barth out. Others asked Barth to take back his remark and to show some civility.

When calm returned, Barth spoke again and said that, actually, he meant what he had said. This was the situation between him and the German Christians. He'd been saying it for nine months. "It is not a matter of persons, it is a matter of fact. The German Christian cause is false and rotten to the core. One can only be for it or against it. And as far as people go, if we are to get them to abandon this false and rotten cause, we must be completely hard and completely cold about it. Anything else would not be love."

During the next hour, Barth sketched an alternate memorandum, but it was so watered down by the other delegates that it proved useless. In the ensuing meeting with Hitler, in which Barth did not participate, church representatives were so intimidated that they could not find any words to oppose Hitler to his face.[3]

Some Protestants refused to be cowed and began organizing themselves in new ways. Free synods—church gatherings held without the permission of official church governing bodies—began meeting in early 1934. These synods were held separately under the auspices of the Lutheran, Reformed, or United churches. They were organized primarily to protest Bishop Müller's heavyhanded leadership and to guard the church's doctrine from the assaults of "positive Christianity." The target was not the Nazis but the German Christians.

The churches that participated in these free synods were called "Confessing churches," and they were located mostly in northern Germany. They didn't view themselves as starting a separate church; instead, they asserted that they—not Müller and the German Christian establishment—were the legitimate church. But as time went on there developed two distinct churches: the Confessing Church and the German Christian Church (though some congregations remain mixed).

The separate synods joined forces at the end of May 1934, gathering in the city of Barmen. Twenty-six provincial churches were represented, with 138 delegates in attendance. All the delegates were questioned ahead of time to make sure that no German Christians were present. Those gathered wanted to declare their common faith in light of the current situation and to organize themselves for the ongoing resistance.

Karl Barth and two Lutheran theologians were assigned the task of writing the declaration. They gathered for lunch and then the two Lutherans took a siesta. Barth couldn't sleep. He later said, "I revised the text of the six statements, fortified by strong coffee and one or two Brazilian cigars." By the time the other theologians woke up, the six articles were written. With only minor variations, the declaration was submitted to the delegates.

The delegates listened in quiet reverence as the Barmen Declaration was read aloud. The vote to accept it was unanimous, and afterwards the delegates spontaneously broke out singing the hymn "All Praise and Thanks to God."

The Sufficiency of Christ

The heart of the Barmen Declaration consists of six theses. Each begins with a biblical quotation, followed by a positive theological affirmation, and then by the rejection of a false teaching of the German Christians. The first thesis is the most important and should be quoted in full:

> "I am the way, and the truth, and the life; no one comes to the Father, but by me" (John 14:6). "Truly, truly, I say to you, he who does not enter the sheepfold by the door, but climbs in by another way, that man is a thief and a robber. . . . I am the door; if anyone enters by me, he will be saved" (John 10:1, 9).
>
> Jesus Christ, as he is attested for us in Holy Scripture, is the one Word of God which we have to hear and which we have to trust and obey in life and in death.

We reject the false doctrine, as though the church could and would have to acknowledge as a source of its proclamation, apart from and besides this one Word of God, still other events and powers, figures and truths, as God's revelation.[4]

This is a clear attack on the German Christians who believed that the "doctrines" of National Socialism and the leadership of Adolf Hitler were also God's revelation to the church. The German Christians would not deny that Jesus Christ should continue to guide the church. But they felt that the Word of God needed to be interpreted in light of unfolding historical events. Barmen said "No!" to this compromise.

The second, third, and fourth articles clarified the unique and exclusive nature of faith in Jesus Christ, as well as rejecting the dictatorial leadership of Bishop Müller. The fifth article turned to the relation of church and state:

"Fear God. Honor the emperor" (1 Peter 2:17).

Scripture tells us that, in the as yet unredeemed world in which the Church also exists, the State has by divine appointment the task of providing for justice and peace. [It fulfills this task] by means of the threat and exercise of force, according to the measure of human judgment and human ability. The Church acknowledges the benefit of this divine appointment in gratitude and reverence before him. It calls to mind the Kingdom of God, God's commandment and righteousness, and thereby the responsibility both of rulers and of the ruled. It trusts and obeys the power of the Word by which God upholds all things.

We reject the false doctrine, as though the State, over and beyond its special commission, should and could become the single and totalitarian order of human life, thus fulfilling the Church's vocation as well.

We reject the false doctrine, as though the Church, over and beyond its special commission, should and could appropriate the characteristics, the tasks, and the dignity of the State, thus itself becoming an organ of the State.[5]

Both Nazi totalitarianism and German Christian nationalism are the objects of this thesis. The two rejections here make clear the absolute separation of church and state, and they boldly criticize the current situation in which God and country, church and state had been mixed in extraordinary ways.

None of Hitler's crimes are mentioned in the Barmen Declaration, nor is anything said about how the Nazis were treating the Jews. The Jewish question—except as it touched on the rights of the church—was still not an issue to the Confessing Church or to Barth.

Decades later, Barth admitted a failure here. In a letter to Eberhard Bethge, the biographer of Bonhoeffer, Barth said, "I myself have long felt guilty that I did not make this problem [the Jewish question] central, at least in public." But, as Barth recognized, given the times, "a word to that effect would not have found general agreement." Most of the pastors, like pastors in general, did not see themselves as politicians, nor did they believe that their call was to speak out on politics. Add to that the Lutheran tradition of acquiescing to political authority, and it's clear that Barth was correct in his assessment. Still, he said, "That I was caught up in my own affairs somewhere else is no excuse for my not having properly fought for this cause."

The Barmen Declaration, then, may not have been everything, but it was something. It was one of a tiny handful of public statements made anywhere in the country, by any association, group, or faith, that openly defied the Nazi regime. It required courage to attend the conference as well as sign the declaration.

The significance of the declaration for Barth was that "it was necessary at that time for all the Evangelical [Protestant] churches and congregations in Germany to resist and attack the assimilation and alienation threatened by the German Christians. The Church had to be strengthened by a reconsideration of its presuppositions and summoned to join battle boldly and confidently." If taken seriously, "it meant a purification of the church not only from the new natural theology which was specifically under discussion, but from all natural theology."

Reverberations

It was in this context that Barth felt compelled, in the fall of that year, to shout his decisive "Nein!" to Emil Brunner's book *Nature and Grace*. The book was an argument for natural theology. Brunner believed, for example, that the church's proclamation must seek a "point of contact" in humankind, some human quality or reality in creation that could point people to God. Barth believed that God needs no point of contact other than that which he himself establishes in the preaching moment. God does not rummage around the human situation looking for something we understand and then make himself known in that entity. No, God manifests himself and his truth independent of any quality inherent in human beings.

For Barth, natural theology was the fundamental theological problem of the German Christians. They were enamored with a variety of points of contact—history, race, and the political enthusiasm of the moment, for example—which they said revealed God at work in the world. Barth thought this amounted to idolatry, mistaking the creation for the Creator. He believed Brunner was joining forces with "the false movement of thought by which the church is threatened today, and at the decisive point." He said he spoke sharply against Brunner because "Brunner is closer to me, and I think that he is closer to the Bible. So at present he seems to me much more dangerous."

The breach with Brunner shows again how Barth lost even close friends during these years. It would be some time before they were reconciled.

The Barmen synod would turn out to be the high point in the life of the Confessing Church. At the next Confessing synod, the governing council was expanded and an executive board established. But over the next few months, internal wrangling over how exactly to relate to the state resulted in a coup by the more conservative faction, which wanted to be more conciliatory toward the state. They did this to ensure the church's independence, but Barth believed they were gutting the force of the Barmen Declaration. As a result, Barth participated less and less in the deliberations of the Confessing Church.

Despite divisions and some waffling, many members of the Confessing Church suffered for their bold stand against Hitler. The most famous were Martin Niemöller, who was imprisoned, and Dietrich Bonhoeffer, who suffered imprisonment and death. Many lesser-known pastors were fired, transferred, or drafted into the military.

Barth had already started to pay his own price. At the end of April 1934, before the Barmen synod, he had been summoned for a long cross-examination by the Ministry of Cultural Affairs regarding a critical comment he had made some months earlier. As a result, he was put under "city arrest." At the end of May, his son Christoph had to flee Germany because of a remark he had made that had been discovered by the secret postal censorship.

On November 7, 1934, Barth was asked, for the last time, to give the required oath of loyalty to Hitler. This had been required of professors since August 1933, when Hitler had combined the offices of chancellor and president. Barth had managed to avoid a confrontation on the issue, but he could no longer. "I did not refuse to give the official oath," he later said, "but I stipulated an addition to the effect that I could be loyal to the Führer only with my responsibilities as an Evangelical Christian."

With that, Barth was suspended from all teaching duties. Barth never forgot how, on the day before his suspension, he and his students sang together:

O may this bounteous God
Through all our life be near us,
With ever joyful hearts
And blessed peace to cheer us.
And keep us in his grace,
And guide us when perplexed,
And free us from all ills
In this world and the next.

The students showed up at the lecture room the next day only to find the doors locked. Charlotte von Kirschbaum told them the news of the suspension. When, in December, a substitute professor was presented to teach the class, one student courageously read a declaration signed by two hundred of his classmates: "We must reject the continuation of Professor Karl Barth's lectures and classes . . . by a substitute." As expected, it changed nothing.

Barth was then called to appear before a tribunal. "Three judges sat opposite me and looked at me with serious, mistrustful faces," he wrote. "And a bold young lawyer sat beside me and took great pains to demonstrate that it was not as bad as all that. But everything took its inevitable course."

During the session, Barth quoted from the *Apology* of Socrates and argued that the church's particular task is to remind the state that another authority stands over and above it. This in fact is the church's duty to the state. Barth said he was only doing his duty on behalf of the state. If the judges could assure him that there was no question of totalitarianism, he might be able to sign the oath. But lacking that, they should realize that they were making Hitler into a god and breaking the first commandment, against idolatry.

Meanwhile, the Reformed Church had determined that, since the oath was made with reference to God, it assumed the qualification that Barth had wanted added. The first court Barth had sat before recognized that. But the mere fact that Barth had thought of this qualification only proved to the authorities that Barth's attitude toward the National Socialist state was dangerous.

Appeals over the next weeks came to naught, and even the governing councils of the Confessing Church, increasingly fearful of alienating the state and risking its independence, refused to publicly support Barth. "I was left in the lurch," he said, "and had to fight the whole battle by myself."

Barth continued to preach and give lectures around the country, but on March 1, 1935, he was entirely forbidden to speak in public. He managed to give one more sermon on March 26, and he continued to speak outside of the country. Finally, on June 14, a Berlin court handed down a surprise judgment: the previous judgment was repealed and Barth was merely fined (20 percent of his annual salary). But eight days later, the Minister of Cultural Affairs dismissed Barth on the basis of the Aryan paragraph of the Law for the Reorganization of the Civil Service.

Knowing that his professional future hung in the balance, Barth and others had already begun seeking new employment opportunities. As it turned out, Barth was dismissed on a Saturday, and by Monday he had received an offer to teach in Basel, Switzerland. He was out of work for one day.

CHAPTER 10

The Basel Years

Wherever there is theological talk, it is always implicitly and explicitly political talk also.

—Karl Barth, 1939

Barth left for Basel immediately with his family and Charlotte von Kirschbaum, who decided to abandon her homeland and her friends to continue to support and assist Barth.[1] Upon leaving Bonn, Barth said, "I have spent the liveliest and richest years of my teaching life here." He was naturally "somewhat depressed" when he returned to Basel, because in part he was "surrounded by narrower questions."

Yes and no. From 1935 to his death in 1968, Barth remained in Basel. There would be lectures and seminars packed with students from all over the world, rich conversations with friends, sparring with theological opponents, traveling, speeches, engagement with all manner of issues. The Barth of the Basel years is the mature Barth, the Barth who believed he had to start all over at the beginning with each new volume of his *Church Dogmatics*—as his method required—but never again would he feel the need to begin again as he did when he rewrote *Romans* or when he set aside the dogmatics he started in Göttingen.

In this sense, Barth's life was "over." There would be no more theological revolutions, no more standing up to antichrists. Instead, we witness the steady production of fourteen volumes of theology that would articulate and expand on hard-won insights. Perhaps the political climate was less dramatic. But it was in Basel that Barth was able to address the largest questions one can imagine, the doctrines of God, of creation, and of reconciliation.

Early in his Basel years, his students included his sons Christoph (who later was to teach Old Testament in Indonesia for many years) and Markus (who later became a professor of New Testament in Dubuque, Iowa, and then in Basel, like his father). This was the period when perhaps Barth's most famous disciple, the Scot Thomas Torrance, sat under his mentor, as did Hans Urs von Balthasar, who became one of the greatest Catholic theologians of the twentieth century.

His early colleagues at Basel included the great Lutheran theologian Oscar Cullmann. His old friend Eduard Thurneysen also taught at Basel—Christian education and preaching—but their intellectual development had moved in different directions since the momentous post–World War I years when they pastored churches near one another and schemed against liberal theology. Inevitably their friendship became less intimate.

Another Basel colleague was his brother Heinrich, who taught philosophy and, according to Karl, was "just about diametrically opposed" to his theology, while Heinrich said Karl was a "man who would brook no opposition. . . . But one has to show him once and for all that even he has his limitations."

Continuing Struggle in Germany

While Barth considered lecturing on theology his "most immediate and important duty," he continued to pay attention to the church's struggle in Germany. He saw more clearly than ever that "the lies and brutality, the stupidity and fear prevalent there were spreading far beyond" the German borders. He continued his vocal opposition to National Socialism "for the sake of the preservation of the true church."

Opposition took many forms. As chairman of the Basel committee of Swiss aid for (exiled) German scholars, he helped procure grants for German students and new jobs for émigrés. He increasingly cared for Jews and Jewish Christians who had been expelled or had escaped from Germany, and he also wrote letters to church leaders in other countries, encouraging them to welcome Jews.

He also wrote letters (some smuggled; some written in code) to Confessing Church leaders, to encourage, advise, and warn. He became increasingly critical of the Confessing Church "for failing to recognize the real danger from the enemy early on and for not opposing the enemy from the start with the Word of God which judges human deceit and injustice." The church rightly fought for its own freedoms, but "it has kept silent . . . over the treatment of Jews, the astonishing treatment of political opponents, the suppression of truth in the press . . . and so much else the Old Testament prophets would certainly have spoken out [against]."[2]

In years to come, Barth widened the scope of his critique: "If I reproach myself over anything connected with my years in Germany," he later wrote, "it is that because I concentrated so much on my task in theology and in the church, and because as a Swiss I was somewhat reluctant to involve myself in German affairs, I omitted to give adequate warning about the trends which I could see in the church and the world around me, ominous though they were."[3]

That being said, Barth at the time also wrote, "The Evangelical church was one sector where the system came up against at least some fairly powerful resistance and remained so"—though it was also clear that the pressure was slowly forcing its disintegration.

Dietrich Bonhoeffer visited Barth three times in 1942 on a secret mission for the counter-espionage department of the German government. Barth later recalled, "At that time, Bonhoeffer spoke to me of the plans to form a military government which would first of all halt the German troops . . . on the fronts that they then held in occupied territories, and would deal with the Allies on this basis. I remember very clearly Bonhoeffer's great amazement when I told him that I thought it impossible that the Allies would agree to this."[4]

Barth also published a variety of articles in local outlets to make Swiss Christians aware of the German church struggle. His efforts went to naught. As he put it, "To all appearances, at any rate, the church people of Switzerland are still in a remarkably carefree and undemanding realm." He added sarcastically that they seem "to have only one interest: . . . not to let the German church struggle spill over into our own local churches, which, God be praised, are so peaceful."

The Politics of War

Before and during the war, Barth's political views made him a pariah not only to National Socialist leaders in Germany but to many leaders in Europe, including his homeland.

When Hitler threatened Czechoslovakia in 1938, Barth sent a letter to a Czech leader saying that "now every Czech soldier will stand and fall not only for the freedom of Europe, but also for the Christian church." He called for "armed resistance against armed threats and aggression." When his views became public, the German press denounced him as a "warmonger," and even the leaders of the Confessing Church censured him publicly.

Within weeks of the infamous Kristallnacht ("crystal night"), during which 177 synagogues were burnt and 20,000 Jews were arrested in Germany, Barth gave a lecture in Zurich on "The Church and Today's Political Questions." "Anyone who is in principle hostile to the Jews," he said, "must also be seen as in principle an enemy of Jesus Christ. Antisemitism is a sin against the Holy Spirit."[5]

When he gave a series of lectures in Holland the following March, Barth was asked by his hosts not to speak on political issues. He summarily rejected the advice: "If those countries which are still free resort to such methods for fear of Germany, then we shall soon have a Hitlerite Europe." When asked to speak only on theology, he said, "Wherever there is theological talk, it is always implicitly and explicitly political talk also."

When the Second World War broke out in September 1939, he grieved for the suffering it would cause, especially for the German people, but he also believed it was "the beginning of the end of Hitlerism." He advocated unconditional resistance to Hitler, telling the churches, "For God's sake we may be human and must defend ourselves against the onslaught of manifest inhumanity with the power of despair." While Barth had long endured charges of pacifism (from his opposition to German militarism in World War I), he was now accused of militarism.

He put his money where his theology was in April 1940, when he reported for armed military service. He later wrote, "I had been declared unfit when I was nineteen, but in my fifty-fourth year I was fit . . . and my bedroom now contained a helmet, a complete uniform, a rifle, and a bayonet, etc. so I would be able to go out at any hour of the day or night to decide the issue."[6]

For the rest of the war, Barth was on active duty, on and off, for a couple of weeks at a time. He admitted he was "probably not a very good or dangerous fighter, but still a soldier, armed and drilled." He served 104 days all together, and he remembered standing watch by the Rhine "at darkest midnight, and to protect the Basel reservoir slept on straw, if I slept at all." Once he did not recognize a corp commander and failed to give him a proper salute. For this he was dressed down and threatened with time in the brig.

In the summer of 1942, Barth was deeply moved by the flood of Jewish refugees who swept into Switzerland; at the same time, he was enraged by local Swiss governments. He believed that "today the Jewish question is virtually the question for statements of Christian belief," so when the government of Berne severely restricted Jewish immigration, he wrote, "The Rhine will not wash away our guilt for having turned away ten thousand refugees and having treated unworthily those whom we did accept."

His arguments for government support of refugees resonate today with many Christian advocates of refugee resettlement: "First, the Christian reason: the fugitives are our concern; not *although* they are Jews but *precisely because* they are Jews and as such physical brethren of our savior. Secondly, the national reason: the fugitives do us the honor of seeing our country as a last stronghold of justice and mercy. . . . And lastly, the human one: we see in fugitives what we have so far, by a miracle, been spared."[7]

Such outspokenness won Barth few friends in the Swiss government. Starting in 1941, he was banned from writing and speaking politically in Switzerland, and he later learned that his phone had been tapped by the police during the war years. (In fact, his attacks on the Swiss government, before, during, and after the war, created such tension that no Swiss government officials attended his funeral in 1968, though many of them did attend the funeral of theologian Karl Jaspers a few months later.)

Some thought Barth flip-flopped when the war ended, at least regarding his attitude toward Germany. As the war was coming to a close, he said that Germans now needed "friends in spite of everything." Paraphrasing Matthew 11:28, he wrote, "Come to me you unlovely creatures, you evil Gestapo blackguards, you sorry compromisers and collaborationists, you sheep who now have run so patiently and dumbly for so long behind your so-called leader. Come to me, you guilty ones and you connivers! . . . I can only see that you are finished, and for good or ill you must begin again. I will refresh you. Now I will begin again with you from scratch."[8]

Such views didn't sit well with the Swiss, who felt Barth was being too friendly, nor with German refugees, who believed Barth was being too radical. But Barth had earlier specified that "Christians in every country should understand that the war was not against the people of Germany but against the dangerous usurpers in their midst." Even after the war, he said more than once that "every German must take responsibility for what had happened since 1933." But he also recognized that the Germans had experienced their judgment, and it was now a moment for mercy.

We must remember that, in the midst of all this political activism before and during the war, Barth was steadily working away at his *Church Dogmatics*. These years saw the publication of (in their later English titles) volume I/2 (*The Doctrine of the Word of God*); II/1 (*The Doctrine of God*, part 1); and II/2 (*The Doctrine of God*, part 2). This is not to mention a number of "smaller" theological works.

Barth was true to his word when he said that he was involved with politics precisely because he was a theologian first. It's also the reason he felt compelled *not* to return to Germany after the war. He later wrote, "The problem of German reconstruction seemed to me personally to be so vast, and made so complicated . . . that I saw myself faced with an alternative: either to return to Germany for good and devote what time and strength remain to me completely and exclusively to German problems and tasks; or to keep on with my real work—namely the continuation and possibly the completion of my *Church Dogmatics*." In the end, the *Dogmatics* won the argument.

He did return to Bonn in the late spring and early summer of 1946 to give a series of lectures based on the Apostles' Creed. The lectures were held in "the semi-ruins of the once stately Kurfursten Schoss in Bonn," he wrote in the introduction to *Dogmatics in Outline*, the book that these lectures became. The lectures started at 7 a.m. and opened with a hymn "to cheer us up." By 8 a.m., they heard the noise of the demolition crane. Believers and unbelievers attended the lectures, and Barth said that "several times during these weeks I was asked, 'Aren't you aware that many people at these lectures are not Christians?' I always laughed and said, 'It makes no difference to me.' It would be quite dreadful if the faith of Christians aimed at separating men and cutting them off from each other. It is in fact the strongest motive for bringing men together and uniting them."[9]

Ecumenical Work

After the war, Barth stuck his toes in the waters of the burgeoning movement to unite Christians across the world. He was invited to give an opening speech at the First Assembly of the World Council of Churches (WCC). At first he turned down the offer, but he was eventually persuaded by some of its leaders. While instinctually suspicious of ecumenical efforts, he was convinced that the efforts were "interesting and important."

The theme of the First Assembly was "Man's Disorder and God's Design," which Barth characteristically reversed: he believed that "we should speak first of God's design and only then of man's disorder." He was critical of the preparatory studies, which suggested that Christians

> ought to achieve what God alone can accomplish and what he will accomplish completely by himself. . . . We shall not be the ones who change this wicked world into a good one. God has not abdicated his lordship over us. . . . All that is required of us is that in the midst of the political and social disorder of the world, we should be his witnesses. We shall have our hands full simply in being that.[10]

He also took part in a preparatory study for the WCC Assembly at Evanston in 1954, which was chaired by Reinhold Niebuhr. At one point, Niebuhr decided to set aside discussion of eschatology; Barth became angry and was ready to storm home. A Japanese delegate convened a meeting between Barth and Niebuhr, but Barth nonetheless returned to Basel "with very mixed impressions" and doubtful "whether I should continue. The Anglo-Saxons, the ecumenical laughter, the eternal balancing of the various points . . . all this finally tired me out."

Barth certainly did not have the personality with which ecumenical discussions thrive, a calm in the face of substantive disagreements. Barth didn't mind disagreements, but he felt they should be expressed as such, and with passion.

Once, in a discussion between Barth and theologian Hans von Campenhausen in a conference on East-West relations, Von Campenhausen burst out in anger at Barth for suggesting that those who disagreed with his views were not sincere or were not Christians. To this Barth replied, "Why don't you put forward your view with the same (Christian) commitment?"

Yet, despite his seeming dogmatism, he could readily make fun of himself and tell a good story on himself. In a celebration of the sixtieth birthday of pastor/activist Martin Niemöller (with whom Barth shared many political views), Barth described an imaginary conversation between them:

Barth: "Martin, I'm surprised that you almost always get the point despite the little systematic theology that you've done!"

Niemöller: "Karl, I'm surprised that you almost always get the point despite the great deal of systematic theology you've done!"[11]

Postwar Politics

The immediate postwar years in Europe saw the Soviet Union annexing, or converting into Soviet Socialist Republics, the countries the Soviets had captured as they drove the German army from Central and Eastern Europe. In a matter of a few years, new satellite states rose in Poland, Bulgaria, Hungary, Czechoslovakia, Romania, Albania, and East Germany.

By 1948, Western observers had become alarmed as these developments unfolded. Given Barth's passionate resistance to National Socialist totalitarianism, many began to wonder why he failed to speak out with equal vehemence against communist totalitarianism. Theologian Emil Brunner and other Swiss critics publicly asked Barth why he did not "issue a call to oppose communism and make a Christian confession" as he had done against National Socialism. This became a recurring and intensive critique of Barth for years.

But Barth did not think communism was much of a threat or temptation in the West, certainly not compared to how Germans were tempted to make an idol of National Socialism. Essentially Barth's view, as expressed in *Theologische Existenz "heute"* (Theological Existence "Today") was this: "I am against all fear of communism. A nation which has a good conscience, whose social and democratic life is in order, need have no fear of it. Much less the church, which is sure of the gospel of Jesus Christ."

He elaborated his views in a lecture, "The Church between East and West," in February 1949. He spoke sternly to "those who are very passionately interested in the East-West question but little or not at all in the church." The Eastern and Western blocs were based on a conflict of power and ideology, but the church should not take sides in such a conflict. "The way of the community of Jesus Christ in the present" has to be "another, third way of its own."[12]

Barth's "third way" was a plea for peace and against the Cold War. But it also meant a definite No to anticommunism: "Not that I have any inclination toward Eastern communism, in view of the face it has presented to the world," he wrote a friend. "I decidedly prefer not to live within its sphere and do not wish anyone else to be forced to do so."

At the same time, he concluded, "But I do not see that either politics or Christianity require or even permit the conclusions which the West has drawn with increasing sharpness. . . . The churches have injured the cause of the gospel by the largely thoughtless manner in which they have identified the gospel . . . with the badly planned and ineptly guided cause of the West."

He also wrote, "*Anti* means 'against.' God is not against, but for men. The communists are men too. God is also for the communists. So a Christian cannot be against the communists but only for them. To be for the communists does not mean to be for communism. I am not for communism."[13]

Given what we know today about the tyranny of Joseph Stalin particularly (who was responsible for the deaths of between six and nine million of his own people),[14] in retrospect Barth does seem naïve on this issue. One cannot help but think that his political sympathies with socialism, born in him during his first pastorate, shaped his views here.

After the Soviet repression of the Hungarian revolt in 1956, Barth said that communism had "pronounced its own verdict on itself" in Hungary. But still he exhorted that the West should take the beam out of its own eyes first. In the face of stormy criticism, including that from political realist Reinhold Niebuhr, Barth mostly refused to respond. He continued to preach "Do not be afraid," and said, "Anyone who does not want communism—and none of us do—should take socialism seriously."

His objection to atomic weaponry better stands the test of time. On Good Friday, 1948, he endorsed an appeal by German scientists and the humanitarian missionary Albert Schweitzer. Barth said, "People in both East and West should rise up against the madness which is in evidence here. We are concerned with life. We are concerned with people." In June of that year, in a telegram to Radio Warsaw, he called on the world powers to renounce their atomic weapons, unilaterally if necessary. "Atomic war cannot be a just war in any sense," he said. "It can only be universal annihilation."[15]

Final Theological Efforts

In all this, Barth continued to concentrate on his *Dogmatics*. During each semester, he said he had "to produce at least eight manuscript pages of extremely complicated thought each day, in a state ready for the publisher." It took him thirty to forty hours of preparation for four hours of lectures. As he told a group of pastors, "My life and work has always been much more burdensome than some people might now imagine."

As he aged, he found that the lectures took "much, much more out of me than they used to." He worked on them all morning and early evening, and even on days he usually took off, Wednesdays and Saturdays. This included editing copy up to fifteen minutes before he was to give the afternoon lecture, after which the manuscript was handed over to the publisher.

During the later 1940s and 1950s (again in addition to smaller theological works), he produced *Church Dogmatics* III in four parts (*The Doctrine of Creation*), and into the early 1960s the three parts of volume IV (*The Doctrine of Reconciliation*).

He did not want his *Dogmatics* to become fixed doctrinal teaching: the project was not "a house," but "an introduction to a way which must be followed." He had no interest in starting a school, and he once said, in a conversation with youth chaplains, "If there are 'Barthians,' I myself am not among them."[16]

Lurking in the background all the while was his dispute with Rudolf Bultmann and his project of demythologization. In 1941, Bultmann published *New Testament and Mythology*, arguing that we should no longer expect, let alone demand, that Christians accept the "mythical world picture" of the New Testament. Bultmann's most famous line is perhaps: "We cannot use electric lights and radios and, in the event of illness, avail ourselves of modern medical and clinical means and at the same time believe in the spirit and wonder world of the New Testament." Thus we must "demythologize" those parts of the New Testament that seem fanciful to moderns and reinterpret them existentially, as descriptions of human experience of history and the divine.

Barth said that Bultmann's project "left me cold . . . because I found it far too humorless." More to the point, his experience of "modern man" led him to believe that this would not likely help convert him.

He wrote the first volume of *Church Dogmatics* IV, *The Doctrine of Reconciliation*, "with constant attention to the . . . rampaging Bultmann controversy." He believed that volume repudiated Bultmann's ideas. "His name does not appear often," he said in the introduction, "but his arguments have always been in my mind." In the end, Barth said, "I think that one can only demythologize demythologization by a better explanation of what Bultmann and his followers seem to have understood as no more than 'myth' and shudder at with horror again and again."[17]

But Barth knew he was swimming against the stream, as Bultmann's ideas caught fire in the 1950s. "There is no mistaking the fact that Bultmann and his pupils can sail nearer to the wind of the time than I, so I have to be content for my objections to be a source of amazement to many levels of the even younger generation."

Barth continues to be a source of amazement for young and old, of course, but today much more in a positive sense.

Personal Life

During these last decades of his life, Barth suffered the personal sorrows and joys common to the human lot. On June 22, 1941, his son Matthias, who had just begun his theological studies, died from a fall while hiking the Frudenhorn, a mountain of some 11,000 feet at its peak.

In the same years, though, Barth found himself enjoying vacations with his sons Markus and Christoph. He said that in his own family "the problem of the generation gap has played little part—or only a cheerful one." He said, "My grown-up sons are my best comrades—which is not a gift bestowed on every father."

In later years, he found that, among all the preachers he listened to, only the sermons of Markus were "of any use to him." He also liked to hear Markus tell Bible stories to his five children "beautifully and faithfully." He enjoyed his grandchildren, and his interactions with them show us a side of Barth that is often overlooked. "One of them wondered recently," Barth wrote in a letter, "whether the many creases in my face had developed because I spent so much of my life laughing."

As Barth grew older, he became much more appreciative of "all kinds of human delights and pleasures which people tend to rush past . . . at any rate, I did." He enjoyed hiking in the mountains as well as regular trips to the movies, especially to see the films of Marlene Dietrich. At night he read fiction, and he became especially fond of the detective fiction of Dorothy Sayers.

And whatever he was doing, he did it with a pipe filled with tobacco "of the Maryland brand."

He remained a picture of health for the most part. We must recall that the year after World War II ended, he was already sixty years old. The bulk of his *Church Dogmatics*—and all the other activities he engaged in—took place after that.

He did have a setback after the winter semester 1951–52, when he found himself exhausted and was diagnosed with diabetes. He soon recovered by going on a strict diet, although he exclaimed to one son, "How glad I would be to be rid of noodles!"

He also made an effort to keep himself in shape. He took a cold shower every morning, slept with the window wide open all year long, did deep-breathing exercises in the evening and exercises in the morning—which he called "dogmatics in movement." He treated himself to jelly and to a variety of vitamins. He observed all the instructions from his doctors, for whom he was thankful, especially since his doctors didn't question his pipe smoking.

Upon the celebration of his seventieth birthday in 1956, he said in a letter to his sons, "I feel like an old weathered fir tree, withered by the sun, rain, wind, and occasionally struck by lightning, bearing the inscription of all kinds of passersby on its bark, but still standing in the same place."

"It is of course many years since I rode horseback through field and wood," he added. "Climbing uphill no longer tempts me. And even the speed with which I work at my desk has become perceptibly slower." Still, "this move toward idleness (and possible decay) is not yet due," in large part because "The *Church Dogmatics* is the decisive factor in the preservation of my physical condition; it cries out to be completed and does not allow my head to hang or my hands to rest. . . . How long things can remain so is another question."[18]

CHAPTER 11

Church Dogmatics—the Word of God

*Even the smallest, strangest, simplest, or obscurest among the
biblical witnesses has an incomparable advantage over even the
most pious, scholarly, and sagacious latter-day theologian.*
—Karl Barth, *An Introduction to Evangelical Theology*

Before we conclude Barth's life, we should spend two chapters
exploring what he spent the bulk of his time writing in these
later years, his *Moby Dick*, the *Church Dogmatics*. An introductory biography, of course, cannot begin to summarize the theology of Karl
Barth in a chapter or two. When Geoffrey Bromiley, the translator
of the *Dogmatics*, tried merely to outline the nearly 9,000 pages of
the *Church Dogmatics*, with hardly an interpretive and explanatory
comment, it took him 278 pages to do so.[1] In this volume, I want
to simply explore two uniquely Barthian doctrines and explain
why I've found them helpful, and so suggest why Barth's theology
might become a resource for evangelical pastors and teachers. Not
by coincidence, these two themes are not only unique to Barth but
also are themes that have been most controversial to evangelicals.

But before we get to the first theme—the Word of God—we
need to understand Barth's starting point in theology, because it
not only was fresh for his day but remains relevant today.

Barth began his *Church Dogmatics* in Bonn as a revision of two
earlier attempts. While at Münster, Barth had made a second stab

at dogmatics, publishing the first of a proposed three-volume work in 1927. Almost immediately he was unhappy with what he had written. He was still groping with what he wanted to say and how he wanted to say it. In the end, he determined this:

> In these years I had to learn that Christian doctrine, if it is to merit its name, and if it is to build up the Christian church in the world as it needs to be built up, has to be exclusively and consistently the doctrine of Jesus Christ. Jesus Christ is the living Word of God spoken to us men. . . . I have discovered that by concentrating on this point, I can say everything far more clearly, unambiguously and simply, in accordance with the church's belief, and yet far more freely, openly, and comprehensively than I could ever have said it before.[2]

One thing that solidified his theme and method was his study of Anselm of Canterbury in 1930–31. After reading Anselm, Barth believed more deeply than ever that it wasn't his job to convince readers of the reality of God or the truth of the Christian faith through rational proofs or convincing arguments. Nor did he think it necessary to know who God is and what he is like before one believes. No, just the opposite: one can know nothing of God unless God reveals himself. It is faith in God that leads to understanding, as Anselm said. And, of course, faith is nothing less than a gift of God.

Thus the beginning of the *Dogmatics* departs from the dogmatic method of Barth's day. Most theologies begin with the prolegomena, introductory remarks in which the theologian gives a philosophical defense of his or her method, answers possible objections, and explains core assumptions. The problem with prolegomena, Barth said, is that they can become pan-legomena, that is, remarks that not merely begin but go on forever and ever, always clearing one's throat but never saying anything. The other problem, especially for Barth, is that most prolegomena ground theology in philosophical assumptions that are alien to the Bible, such as Hegelianism or existentialism. Too many theologians use philosophy to justify theology's existence, which Barth thought to be a major mistake.

In Barth's "prolegomena," he begins by doing theology. There is no philosophical or empirical basis for doing theology, he says. As he first noted in his *Romans*, given who God is and who we are, talk about God in itself is impossible—unless God breaks through the impasse. Talk about God is possible not because there is some human point of contact or some divine spark within men and women, but only because God has made it possible by revealing himself in Jesus Christ. God has been merciful enough to endow human language with the ability to point to the Word of God, and to send us his Holy Spirit to illumine that Word.

Thus dogmatics begins with an act of faith: trust that God has in fact revealed himself in Jesus Christ. And so dogmatics seeks to understand who God is and what God has revealed and is revealing by looking to his Word. The theologian, along with the church he or she serves (for all theology, says Barth, is done not as an academic discipline but to build up the church), sits under the authority of the Word and does theology as an act of faith and obedience to that Word.

The Word of God

For Barth, the Word of God comes to us in a threefold reality: the preached Word, the written Word, and the revealed Word.

The preached Word is an event that creates hearers; through preaching, the Word comes alive in hearers' lives. When this happens, the Word can truly be said to be not merely a human word of a human preacher but a divine Word in which the very presence and power of Christ are mediated to us.

"Witness" is a key word for Barth when it comes to both preaching and Scripture. Witnesses point away from themselves. The biblical authors "do not want to offer and commend themselves to the Church, and especially not their own particular experience of God and relationship to God."[3] Preaching, like Scripture, does not have authority intrinsically, but only insofar as it points to Jesus Christ, the revealed Word. Thus the written Word, the second form, is the material ground for all preaching. Scripture is a recollection of the revelation that points to the life, death, and resurrection of Jesus Christ. Scripture then is the canon, the collection of books by which the church governs its life and talk. Furthermore, the books that constitute the church's canon were not created or selected by the church but have been imposed on the church by Scripture itself through the Holy Spirit. So, even in regard to the canon, the church sits under Scripture and not over it.

The third form of the Word of God is the revealed Word, in particular, Jesus Christ. This is the Word who became flesh and dwelt among us, dying and rising for us, the Word who continues to make himself known today in and through preaching and Scripture.

In regard especially to the second form of the Word of God, Scripture, Barth says some things that have understandably made evangelicals squirm.

First, Barth emphasizes that Jesus Christ, the Word made flesh, is the true act of God, and Scripture is but the human record of that act. Thus Jesus Christ is the definitive Word while Scripture is merely human beings' word about Christ. The Bible's "truth, power, and validity" rest not in the Bible itself but in that it is a witness to something else.

Barth says Scripture "is God's Word in so far as God lets it be His Word," insofar as God speaks through it. Therefore, "The Bible . . . becomes God's Word" as we hear it.[4] The Bible does not become God's Word because we read it in faith, but because through the Holy Spirit it becomes revelation for us. As Barth puts it, "The Bible is God's Word to the extent that God causes it to be His Word, to the extent that He speaks through it."[5]

Some churches have picked up on this idea; instead of prefacing a Scripture reading with "Listen to the Word of God," they say, "Listen for the Word of God." In such settings, evangelicals have been known to whisper, "Because it might be there, and it might not!" The joke gets at one evangelical concern about Barth's view of Scripture: one wonders if we can rely on Scripture to be God's Word in any given situation. In his systematic theology, Carl F. H. Henry summarized this understanding of Barth's view: "The Bible is the Word of God, but only at certain instants . . . when God lets the Bible speak to us."[6]

Though this is a common initial reaction to Barth's view of Scripture, a careful reading of Barth shows that things are not that simple with him. As Kevin Vanhoozer notes, "It is especially important in Barth's case to listen to all that he has to say about Scripture," not just in volume I of the *Church Dogmatics* but also in volume II. John Webster, in his introduction to Barth, notes that "the language of witness has a double purpose: it gives full weight to the function of Scripture as the bearer of revelation, and does so without taking away from the fact that the Bible is a collection of human texts."[7] So it is not quite fair to suggest that Barth thinks of the Bible as "merely" a pointer to God's revelation; it is indeed a text through which God shows himself. As Barth says, the Bible "is for us revelation by means of the words of the prophets and apostles written in the Bible, in which they are still alive for us as the immediate and direct recipients of revelation, and by which they speak to us. A real witness is not identical with that which it witnesses, but it sets it before us."[8]

Given this larger understanding, I don't know that traditional evangelical theology has much to argue with. Evangelicals have traditionally agreed that Barth is right to emphasize that the Bible is not a magic book that, in and of itself, has supernatural powers. The Bible's truths need to come alive for us by the dynamic work of the Holy Spirit, or else it just reads like any other book.

Furthermore, evangelicals would affirm that Jesus Christ, not the Bible, is the way, the truth, and the life. Jesus Christ, not the Bible, died and rose and lives in us through the Holy Spirit. The Bible is indeed a record or witness of how God has revealed himself to us in Christ. Likewise, evangelicals affirm that Scripture is the work of human beings, using human language and grammar to talk about a revelation that happened once and for all in Christ. It is a book that can be studied with the same tools used to understand any other human book. But most evangelicals, in reading Barth, want to emphasize something that Barth seems to merely allude to, that there is something given in the biblical text as such that is "infallible" or "inerrant."

This is one area where evangelicals especially stumble when reading Barth: his emphatic rejection of biblical inerrancy or infallibility. He goes so far as to say that the Bible contains historical, scientific, and even theological errors! It was compiled by many men over thousands of years—how could it be infallible?

Evangelicals, of course, want to ask Barth how it is possible for us then to trust it to be a means of revelation if, in fact, it contains errors, even in matters of theology. His answer, for better or worse, is his *Church Dogmatics*. A summary of how Barth understands and actually uses Scripture will have to do for now.

A Dynamic Word

First, beginning with his commentary on Romans, Barth had an allergic reaction to anything that smacks of idolatry. For him, to say that the Bible is inerrant is to use a predicate that applies only to God. It is to make the Bible equal to God. Barth vehemently rejects idolatry in any form, but especially when it comes in the guise of religion. In fact, for Barth, the fact that the Bible has errors brings all the more glory to God, for God is shown to use this fallible book to reveal himself to people. As evangelical theologian Kevin Vanhoozer puts it, for Barth, "the miracle is not that the human authors spoke infallibly, but rather that God uses fallible human words to speak his infallible Word."[9]

Second, central to Barth's theology is the notion that God is active. Barth's theology is full of the language of *occurrence, happening, event, decision,* and *act.* When he thinks of God, he thinks not in terms of a being who has a static substance, simple and immovable because he is already perfect. The static God is not the God of the Bible, whom Barth sees as always on the move, always acting, and acting on and for his people. It is impossible to talk about God except in his ongoing relations. Thus Barth is leery of language that suggests that the Word of God is static, that truths lie in it passively, truths we can study and manipulate with the tools of exegesis guided by human intellect.

Third, Barth is anxious to preserve God's freedom. He doesn't want to tie God down to the literal words of a book or to say that God is somehow obligated to speak through these words every time they are read. He wants to remind us that we serve not a dead, legalistic word, but a *living* God who is free to reveal himself when and where he will.

In addition, we need to put Barth's comments about biblical inerrancy in a larger context. The paradox is that, when it comes to using the Bible, Barth seems to treat the Bible as if it were inerrant! That's hyperbole, to be sure, and a phrase Barth would decidedly reject. But when he exposits the Bible, he does so as if it is completely trustworthy and authoritative. He never dismisses a passage as being in error. He has no interest in undermining the authority of the Bible—in fact, it is Barth who rescued the Bible from the relativistic Scripture reading of nineteenth-century liberalism. In his day, liberals accused him of being a biblical literalist! Barth said his *Church Dogmatics* "is best read as a set of conceptual variations upon scriptural texts and themes." Thus Barth cites more Scripture than any other theologian in the history of theology, some 15,000 times in the *Church Dogmatics.* All this is why Kenneth Kantzer, former editor of *Christianity Today,* appreciated Barth and said, "Evangelicals have much to learn from his constant and faithful appeal to Scripture."[10]

For Barth, as it is for evangelicals at their best, the Bible is a dynamic book. And most evangelicals recognize the impossibility of reading Scripture as a book of infallible science or history— they recognize that there are sometimes competing versions of the same stories, some anomalies, and even contradictions that are not easily resolved. That being said, they continue to believe that it is a book that can be trusted to guide us infallibly in matters of faith and practice, if for no other reason than that it points time and again to God's action in Jesus Christ. Again Vanhoozer on Barth: "He is unequivocal on the matter of the Bible's authority over the church"[11]—and even over theology. As Barth put it, "Even the smallest, strangest, simplest, or obscurest among the biblical witnesses has an incomparable advantage over even the most pious, scholarly, and sagacious latter-day theologian."[12]

For reasons historical and theological, evangelicals will likely retain the words "inerrant" and "infallible" to talk about the Bible to signal that it is an absolutely trustworthy book when it comes to showing us who God is and what he commands. That being said, increasingly many evangelical theologians today are asking whether "inerrancy" brings with it more problems than it solves. It is a word and idea grounded in Enlightenment rationalism and thus is an attempt to build confidence in the Bible on the basis of rationalism. That, as Barth and many others would argue, is a shaky foundation indeed.

Furthermore, as many evangelicals themselves admit, sometimes in using such language we are trying to defend, protect, and preserve the authority of the Bible, as if that sort of thing were up to us. On top of that, we're tempted to create systems of interpretation and rules of exegesis, as if we can confine Scripture to some human system. Barth reminds us that Scripture is not something we preserve and manipulate, let alone protect, but the means by which the Word encounters us, preserves us, and, if you will, "manipulates" us—that is, shapes us into the beings we were created to be.

Barth's theology has a way of turning the tables like that. Even when we come to disagree with him, we find we have discovered anew some basic biblical themes, such as that God is God independent of our paltry understanding of him, and that it's less important how we exegete the Word than that the Word first exegetes us.

CHAPTER 12

Church Dogmatics—
Universal Reconciliation

Pardon—by God and therefore unconditionally pronounced and unconditionally valid—that is man's justification. . . . Whether man hears it, whether he accepts it and lives as one who is pardoned is another question.

—Karl Barth, *Church Dogmatics,* IV/1

Another significant theme in Barth is his understanding of redemption, in particular his unique teaching on the doctrine of election. This has been one of the most controversial themes in the history of Protestantism, and Barth attempted to break through the controversy with a fresh approach. Theologians continue to debate whether it is, in fact, more true to Scripture than the alternatives.

In the early church and Reformation eras, election and its counterpoint, reprobation, refer to a teaching that humanity is divided into two groups. God chooses some, the reprobate, to be eternally damned; he chooses others, the elect, to be eternally saved. Up to Barth, the theological discussion of election always centered on *who* was saved, but it created problems when it came to thinking about who did the saving. What type of God is this who arbitrarily saves some and condemns others? Can he truly be loving and just? While some Christians (like the Reformed) have embraced this doctrine, others (like Arminians) have rejected it. The former think it protects the sovereign initiative of God; the latter think it makes God into an arbitrary deity.

Barth's unique approach to election looks not merely at who is elect but at who does the electing. He grounds election not in an arbitrary decision made before the beginning of time but in the gracious character of the One who does the electing. Barth focuses the sum total of all the elect and all the reprobate down to one person: Jesus Christ. From all eternity, Christ is both the only one who elects and the only one who is elected. As such, he is also the only one chosen for the full measure of wrath against sin, and yet, at the same time, he is the only one elected for eternal salvation. So, the election and reprobation of men and women can be understood only in a secondary sense. In taking on human flesh, Jesus Christ takes on our humanity and thus becomes one with us. In his life, death, and resurrection, then, he acts also for us. Our destiny is grounded in Christ, in who he is and what he has done for us. As a substitute for all men and women, he has absorbed the wrath of God against sin and wickedness. As the representative of all men and women, his death reconciles us to God. In the end, if Christ is the representative of humanity, then all humanity is elect. And that means all humanity is forgiven and reconciled.

This naturally leads into a discussion of justification. Barth puts it this way:

> There is not one for whose sin and death He did not die, whose sin and death He did not remove and obliterate on the cross, for whom He did not positively do the right, whose right He has not established. There is not one to whom this was not addressed as His justification in His resurrection from the dead. There is not one whose man He is not, who is not justified in Him. There is not one who is justified in any other way than in Him—because it is in Him and only in Him that an end, a bonfire, is made of man's sin and death. . . . Again, there is not one who is not adequately

and perfectly and finally justified in Him. *There is not one* whose sin is not forgiven sin in Him.[1]

Barth does not marginalize the biblical teaching on God's wrath and judgment. This is not the sentimental gospel of liberalism, where God is, after all, a reasonable and kind fellow who merely overlooks our sins, a God who will *of course* forgive! No. For Barth, pardon is indeed the positive side of God's sentence. But the negative side of the sentence is God's judgment "that we are these proud creatures, that I am the man of sin, and that this man of sin and therefore I myself am nailed to the cross and crucified (in the power of the sacrifice and obedience of Jesus Christ in my place), that I am therefore destroyed and replaced, that as the one who has turned to nothingness I am done away in the death of Jesus Christ."[2]

But in the end, pardon does not depend on one's response to Christ, that is, it doesn't depend even on faith. Instead, *total* pardon is objectively accomplished in Jesus Christ on behalf of all of humankind.

Universalism?

Barth pushes these ideas so hard that some have accused him of universalism—the teaching that all people, believers and unbelievers, Christians and pagans, will eventually be saved. About this two things should be said.

First, Barth denied that he was a universalist. Barth so wanted to protect the freedom of God that he couldn't become a universalist. Universalism posits what God will do to and for each individual at the end of time. Barth rejected that as a doctrine that hems God in, so to speak, predicting how God will act based on the logic of some theological principle. Barth's theology was too dynamic to let that happen. "Even though theological consistency might seem to lead our thoughts and utterances most clearly in this direction [universalism], we must not arrogate to ourselves that which can be given and received only as a free gift."[3] Or, as he put it rather more bluntly: "To the man who persistently tries to change the truth into untruth, God does not owe eternal patience and therefore deliverance."[4]

Second, that being said, it is not unfair, given Barth's overwhelming emphasis, to think his theology moves inevitably toward universalism.

The influential Catholic theologian Hans Urs von Balthasar has been deeply influenced by Barth. But in this regard, he thinks Barth is kidding himself:

> Despite these demurrals, Barth's doctrine of election does not leave much room open for possibility. There is something inevitable and necessary in his views. What is definitive in Barth's thought is grace and blessing, and all reprobation and judgment are merely provisional. . . . Actually, given his premises, Barth really cannot discuss this issue in any other way. True, he gives lip service to our inability to survey the full implications of the activity of the Word of God. He speaks of a healthy "inconsistency" in dogmatics. But these are mere words, because he has already immured the idea of an all-encompassing redemption in the very groundwork and foundation of his doctrine of creation.[5]

Theologian Oliver Crisp, in an article entitled "On Barth's Denial of Universalism," makes a number of observations that drive home this point. Barth is not arguing (as traditional Arminians do) that atonement is universal in scope but not in effectiveness; Christ's atonement for Barth is not only *potentially* effective for all but actually effective for all. Consequently, Barth emphasizes salvation as "knowledge" (which comes through faith) that one is *already saved* rather than faith being the means by which salvation is appropriated (as it is in the traditional Reformation formulas). So whereas the Reformers say, "If you repent and believe, you will be saved," Barth says, "You are saved; therefore, believe and repent!" In the end, Crisp makes a strong argument that, despite all his denials, the logic of Barth's theology demands universalism.[6]

Reconciliation and Faith

Insofar as Barth's doctrines of election and justification move in the direction of universalism, of course, evangelicals rightly reject his views. The Bible clearly demonstrates time and again the necessity of a full and free response of faith for us to be reconciled to God. While there are passages that suggest that all will be saved ("For God has consigned all to disobedience, that he may have mercy on all"—Rom. 11:32), others point unequivocally to the eternal destruction of those who rebel against God ("if anyone's name was not found written in the book of life, he was thrown into the lake of fire"—Rev. 20:15).

But many Barthians, both professional theologians and those on the front lines of ministry, are making positive use of Barth's teaching on universal reconciliation, and doing so in the context of a classic understanding of the role of faith. They are setting Barth in historical context, showing that he is not alone, that many orthodox theologians in church history have affirmed universal reconciliation without becoming universalists.

Take Barthian scholar George Hunsinger, who says, "Perhaps no theologian of the church since Athanasius, in whom the strong association of 'in Christ' and 'for all' is consistently present . . . has so consistently tried to do direct justice to the universalistic aspects of the New Testament witness to Jesus Christ as has Barth."[7]

And while Barth repeatedly acknowledged that all human beings are included in the efficacy of the death of Christ, even Barth recognized that living in that reality is another matter: "Pardon—by God and therefore unconditionally pronounced and unconditionally valid—that is man's justification. . . . Whether man hears it, whether he accepts it and lives as one who is pardoned is another question."[8]

How that gets worked out among individuals is left to God. Barth leaves that question open in hope, a position that Hunsinger calls "reverent agnosticism." Hunsinger notes that two points are essential to Barth's understanding of salvation. "First, what took place in Jesus Christ for our salvation avails for all. Second, no one actively participates in him and therefore in his righteousness apart from faith." The first point emphasizes the objective aspect of faith—what God has done in Jesus Christ. The second point has the experiential side of faith in view. The first is determined solely by God; the second does nothing but respond to what God has already accomplished. Thus Hunsinger concludes, "The human act of faith . . . in no way conditions, contributes to, or constitutes the event of salvation. Faith therefore confronts the Savior in sheer gratitude and sheer receptivity (which is not the same as mere passivity), and is itself inexplicable except as a miracle of grace." To reinforce the point, he adds, "The objective validity and efficacy of salvation in Christ by no means eliminates the necessity of actively receiving it in faith. . . . Faith is necessary as the only apt response to the objective reality and efficacy of salvation. It is the response of gratitude, joy, trust, love, and obedience."[9]

Reconciliation and Evangelism

Not just theologians but also some evangelists are taking their cues from Barth, as well as from his disciple T. F. Torrance. As noted earlier, Jeff McSwain was a Young Life leader for years before being dismissed because of his Barthian views.[10] But he remains in youth ministry (having founded Reality Ministries in North Carolina) and continues to preach the gospel of God's universal redemption and the need for a response of repentance and faith.

McSwain began rethinking his approach to ministry as a result of wrestling with the views of Arminians and Five-Point Calvinists. He notes that Arminians resist any theology that would limit God's expansive love on the cross to a few. They find it impossible to believe what Calvinists teach, that Jesus loves everyone but did not die for everyone. On the other hand, Calvinists shake their heads at Arminians because they seem to ignore key biblical passages that speak of Christ's saving work in the past tense—as an accomplished, objective fact. For Calvinists, to say that it is our *faith* that makes Christ's death effectual is to say that salvation rests on our shoulders: salvation is not true until we believe it.

McSwain argues that, like Arminians, Barthians believe that Jesus loves everyone and that he died on the cross for everyone. Like Calvinists, he says Barthians believe that the atoning work of Christ actually accomplished reconciliation and forgiveness for everyone for whom Christ died. He concludes:

> Instead of dismissing Barth, it would behoove evangelicals to consider the possibility that Barth's theology is the most evangelical of all. . . . With a dynamic theology of the Holy Spirit to go along with his robust theology of the cross, Barth knifes through the Gordian Knot of Arminianism and five-point Calvinism, and encourages evangelists to consider a third way, a way of making bold and inclusive claims upon the life of every hearer. That's why I have continued to submit that Barth's proclamation approach, as anticipated by the church fathers Irenaeus and Athanasius, and followed by Dietrich Bonhoeffer and James and T. F. Torrance, provides a worthy hand of theological belonging for Young Life's glove of practical belonging.

McSwain notes a comment of Jim Rayburn, the founder of Young Life, made in 1957 at the Young Life Staff Conference. Rayburn was teaching on 2 Corinthians 5:19, which says that "God was reconciling the world to himself in Christ, not counting men's sins against them." In his teaching, Rayburn said, "Reconciliation. Every single person in the whole wide world is now reconciled to God. . . . It's been true for nearly two thousand years. *I wonder what they* [high school kids] *would do if they knew it.* . . . God has reconciled us, all of us, it's already done."

McSwain points this out not to imply that Rayburn was a universalist but to show that he implicitly accepted what McSwain calls "universal belonging." That is, everyone belongs in the objective, redemptive work of Christ. But this did not mean for Rayburn, and does not mean for McSwain, that people don't have to respond: "Paul's passion for people [was that they] come to *a knowledge of the truth* (cf. 1 Tim. 2:3–6), or what the Bible elsewhere calls repentance (*metanoia*), a radical change of mind that transforms our lives." But when it comes to presenting the gospel to those who don't believe, McSwain says, "Like Rayburn and the Apostle Paul, Barth's proclamation of the gospel began at the starting point of theological belonging for all."

He reiterates Hunsinger's point, above:

> Although we do not create objective truth by our subjective decisions, we may freely participate in objective truth. This happens by the Holy Spirit, appropriately named the Spirit of Truth. With Spirit-filled anticipation, Paul, Rayburn, and Barth all urged their hearers to repent and believe the good news. While perhaps disagreeing with Barth on the nuances of the subjective, Rayburn at the very least refused to arbitrate the truth; in other words, he refused to allow the objective truth to be frittered away in order to make room for subjective response.

As I listen to evangelical preaching and teaching, I would agree that the gospel is often "frittered away in order to make room for subjective response." In many presentations, the preacher makes it sound like our salvation hinges on what *we* do.

This is one reason I am attracted to what Barth teaches here, at least as articulated by people like Hunsinger and McSwain. It helps me as a teacher and preacher to proclaim good news that is really good news—"God really does love you and proved it by dying on the cross for you, reconciling you to himself, forgiving your sins." This good news is not sentimental, as it so often becomes in liberalism. It really does take seriously the gravity of sin, the reality of divine wrath and judgment. The unadulterated good news takes into account the horrible reality of sin. But it is good news with no ifs, ands, or buts. No quid pro quo. No qualifications.

At the same time, this universal redemption is not automatic, as it is in universalism. What universalism and Calvinism have in common is that the fate of every individual person is determined in advance. To me, these views fail to appreciate the mysterious and dynamic nature of our response to God, to which Scripture witnesses from cover to cover. While extolling God's sovereign love and initiative, it also calls us to make decisions in this life, and it says that those decisions have momentous consequences. We are called to repent, that is, to undergo *metanoia*, a complete change of perspective. We are called, and we are told to call others, to decision. That is inescapable in Scripture.

Barth's theology in this regard leans in the Reformed direction, but even Arminians agree that our wills are trapped until the Holy Spirit opens our ears to really hear the gospel; even our response to the good news has to be generated by the power of the Holy Spirit. The Holy Spirit makes it possible for us to grasp the reality of this good news. The Holy Spirit then frees us from the bondage of pride to respond to this invitation. The Holy Spirit makes it possible for us to freely obey Christ.

This Barthian move doesn't solve all theological problems that have always presented themselves at this "moment of decision." It remains a point of contention whether in the moment that the Holy Spirit reveals God's love to us we really can reject it and thus condemn ourselves. And if so, why are only some given irresistible grace? What does it mean to be saved but to reject one's salvation? Many questions still remain.

As do many opinions about Barth's solution—universal reconciliation grounded in God's election. I have read powerful arguments against Barth's views, such as Michael Horton's in his systematic theology, so I'm not ready to say that Barth is the way, the truth, and the life on these matters. But I do think his theology is a fresh approach to a long-standing theological problem, and one that opens up new lines of thought while creating fresh enthusiasm for how we do evangelism. This is another instance where, even when one ends up disagreeing with Barth, he forces one to think more deeply about how utterly gracious God is.

Speaking personally, Barth has helped me talk about the gospel as unquestionable good news while taking seriously the gravity of sin and judgment and the need for a free human response. In my reading of this whole business, it seems that 2 Corinthians 5:19–20 crystallizes the dynamic of God's electing justification and the need for faith:

> In Christ God was reconciling the world to himself, not counting their trespasses against them, and entrusting to us the message of reconciliation. Therefore, we are ambassadors for Christ, God making his appeal through us. We implore you on behalf of Christ, be reconciled to God.

God has reconciled the world to himself through a costly death. And we are implored to be reconciled to God by responding in faith. That to me is about as simple as the gospel gets.

CHAPTER 13

Preacher and Pastor

I also admonish you in all seriousness, don't make a myth out of
me, for the angels will certainly not like that.
            —Karl Barth, circular letter on his seventy-fifth birthday

After the heroic stand against fascist Germany and some deep
thoughts from the monumental *Church Dogmatics*, it seems wise
to end this brief survey by looking at Barth on a more mundane
level. While Barth was changing the course of church history, he
remained a husband and father, a preacher, a pastor, and a friend
to many. At times, Barth's theology can ascend the heights of ab-
straction. At other times, he is dramatic, willful, bombastic, and,
yes, dogmatic! Barth believed that the theologian's duty was to say
what one meant and to say it with conviction. He expected those
he disagreed with to do the same. But there is more to Barth than
theological sparring.

For one, there was his appearance and demeanor. He was on
the tall side, with a high forehead and cheekbones, bushy eyebrows
and pale blue eyes. In his later years, many remarked that he looked
like a casting agency's idea of a German professor—with a shock
of wild hair and horn-rimmed glasses sitting on the tip of his nose.
Theologian Thomas Oden visited him in the hospital in his later
years. Oden wrote, "The most distinct instantaneous impression
was of his wry smile, with his broken teeth, his famous pipe and

bright, twinkly eyes. He radiated friendliness, depth, and warm personal interest in me."[1]

And novelist John Updike noted the paradox of Barth's theology and his lifestyle:

Karl Barth's insistence upon the otherness of God seemed to free him to be exceptionally (for a theologian) appreciative and indulgent of this world, the world at hand. His humor and love of combat, his capacity for friendship even with his ideological opponents, his fondness for his tobacco and other physical comforts, his tastes in art and entertainment were heartily worldly, worldly not in the fashion of those who accept this life as a way-station and testing-ground but of those who embrace it as a piece of God's Creation.[2]

This comment came in a foreword to Barth's book on Mozart, the very worldly composer whose energetic and dynamic music (especially compared to the devout and measured Bach) Barth treasured his entire life. He not only listened to Mozart almost daily, but in Bonn, for example, he played in Mozart string quartets—"discreetly in the background as a viola player," he said. Other interests included English detective novels, riding horses (he said he was a "bad but passionate horseman"),[3] and a fascination with the American Civil War.

One gets a sense of Barth's openness to life in his comments on his visit to America in 1962. In one letter to a relative, he wrote, "All in all, I really like America. The people I have met so far are all so free and open and lively that I can overlook or make allowance for the obvious trash. (Television, which we watched one evening, was a real abomination!) . . . Even to see the flowing traffic on the broad streets is quite a pleasure."[4]

In another, he said, "America, which we have sampled a little in the Midwest, East, and West, is a fantastic affair, a world in which much is astonishingly alike and much astonishingly unlike. When people ask for impressions of America, one's mouth simply closes; there is no knowing where to begin, since generalizations are certainly wide of the mark."[5]

Family

Barth admitted in his later years that, especially when he was feverishly working on *Romans*, "the family had largely lost their father to his desk, as the parish had lost its pastor." He still watched his children grow with "care and delight," and he made sure to participate in their lives as much as he could. For example, he said that every morning he made time to comb his son Christoph's hair "more for my own pleasure than for his gain and satisfaction." And he would entertain his children with stories of "Happy Families," based on people they all knew in Safenwil.[6]

While in Bonn, Barth admitted that it was his wife who "all her life devoted her energies faithfully and zealously" to the work of bringing up the children. And he acknowledged that he was an indulgent parent: "I brought them up on a very long lead—or rather, I hardly brought them up, but let them grow and get on with things." In raising his children, he says, "There were never tensions or scenes between us, but plenty of friendly exchanges which always taught me a lot. . . . And if criticism was due from my side, I certainly never kept it back. But everything tended to happen increasingly on the basis of a free and open friendship."[7]

Barth was not wont to share much regarding his relationship with his wife, Nelly, but as noted earlier, it seems that those severely discomforting years caused by the presence of "Lollo" were eventually forgiven.

Pastor

He may have ended as a theologian, but Barth always remained what he was at the beginning.

While from the start he pursued the intellectual life, he was first committed to being a pastor. In his parish, he not only worked for the rights of the poor but spent time with them. Recalls biographer Eberhard Busch, "Old persons in [the] parish told me when Barth was in Safenwil, it was the first time in a hundred years that there was a Christian pastor who liked the 'little people.' That was their impression."[8]

Clearly, though, Barth saw his role first and foremost as a preacher. Even after he became a theologian, he never stopped preaching, and he continued to hold preaching as the preeminent task of the church. He wrote the *Church Dogmatics* primarily to clarify what the church needed to proclaim, and European preachers eagerly awaited the release of each volume of the *Dogmatics* precisely because his theology helped them preach biblically once again.

Barth may have been a preacher, but apparently he did not care much for liturgy. "Even during my youth," he once wrote, "I had an antipathy to all ceremonial worship. I was aware of always being clumsy before the 'altars' of the German churches where I had to preach." After one occasion when he led worship, a friend told him, "Sermon, first-class; liturgy, fifth-class."[9]

Commenting on Anglican worship, Barth once said, "If the Anglo-Saxons would not make their phylacteries so broad and so long! I went to an Evening Prayer at which the Lord's Prayer was said twice and the Gloria five or six times. I said to them afterwards, 'If I were the good God, I would reply to you in a voice of thunder, 'All right, that will do. I've heard you!'"[10]

While Barth penned his mighty *Dogmatics* Monday through Saturday, he spent many a Sunday in the Basel prison, preaching to the inmates. These sermons are not examples of great preaching, but they do help us see Pastor Barth in action, how he talked about the gospel to ordinary people.

Take his sermon "Saved by Grace," which he preached in August 1955.[11] Some characteristic passages give a flavor:

> Who are we anyway? Let me tell you quite frankly; we are all together great sinners. . . . Sinners are people who in the judgment of God, and perhaps their own consciences, missed and lost their way, who are not just a little, but totally guilty, hopelessly indebted and lost not only in time, but in eternity. . . .
>
> To be saved does not just mean to be a little encouraged, a little comforted, a little relieved. It means to be pulled out like a log from a burning fire. You have been saved! . . .
>
> That God is God, not only almighty, but merciful and good, that he wills and does what is best for us, that Jesus Christ died for us to set us free, that by grace in him, we have been saved—all this need *not* be a concern of our prayers. But to believe, to accept, to let it be true for us, to begin to live with this truth, to believe it not only with our minds and with our lips, but also with our hearts and with all our life, so that our fellow man may sense it, and finally to let our total existence be immersed in the great divine truth, *by grace you have been saved*, this is to be the concern of our prayers. No human being has ever prayed for this in vain. If anyone asks for this, the answer is already being given and faith begins.

As one student of Barth's preaching put it, "This Colossus of a theologian is basically concerned with simple things . . . no one reading Barth can have any doubt . . . [about his] single-hearted devotion to Christ."[12]

Prayer

Barth the preacher believed deeply in the necessity of prayer. Prayer and preaching belong together. Each of his published sermons is preceded by and ended with a prayer. In these prayers, we see, again, the personal and devout side of the theologian. Take the prayer that opened his sermon "Saved by Grace."

> O Lord, our God! Through thy Son, our Lord Jesus Christ, thou hast made us thy children. We have heard thy voice and have gathered here to give thee praise, to listen to thy word, to call upon thee and to entrust to thy care our burdens and our needs. Be thou in our midst and be our teacher—that all our anxiety and despair, all vanity and defiance within us, all our unbelief and superstition may diminish and thy greatness and good may show forth.[13]

Barth believed that when it came to doing theology, "The first and basic act of theological work is prayer." Both the theologian and the preacher, he said, move forward together "in the fellowship of prayer," and the preacher and the hearer "rely on the free grace of God and therefore on prayer." The same applies to our reading and understanding of Scripture, in which "the decisive activity is prayer." If Scripture is to speak to us as the living Word of God, "prayer must have the last word." Through prayer, we acknowledge that the power belongs to God, and not to ourselves.[14]

Many years before, in April 1934, Barth was delivering lectures in Paris when he gave his famous description of theology, which suggests another reason prayer was vital:

> Of all disciplines theology is the fairest, the one that moves the head and heart most fully, the one that comes closest to human reality, the one that gives the clearest perspective on the truth which every disciple seeks. . . . But of all disciplines, theology is also the most difficult and the most dangerous, the one in

which a man is most likely to end in despair, or—and this is almost worse—arrogance.[15]

Retirement Years

In his later years, it became clear that he was not going to complete his *Dogmatics*. To add to his volumes on the doctrines of God, creation, and reconciliation, he wanted to write on the doctrine of redemption. Especially after his retirement, though, he seems to have lost the energy to do that.

He did complete one final section, best known as his work on infant baptism (which he argued against). But after he finished it, he wrote,

> C.D. IV, 4, is being prepared but is far from complete. Eschatology? Friends, do not ask or complain or plague me too much about this. Could it not be written by someone else? Haven't many fine symphonies and buildings and theological *summas* been left unfinished? But I commit these things to God, who knows better than you and I do what is needful for you and possible for me.[16]

In a letter to a friend, he admitted that he suffered from what we would today call depression:

> With many others, especially Lollo, you will naturally tell me I should give myself the more energetically to work on C.D. Yes indeed, if only I had not been gripped by a lassitude bordering on acedia in relation to the whole theological scene. In the face of the thrust of our theological existentialists I increasingly feel only more disgust and abhorrence. . . . Does it make much sense to write a thirteenth and fourteenth volume if I could not stop this deluge with my previous twelve volumes? Are not other and new voices . . . needed to check it? Meanwhile I . . .

sit at a little table in the corner laughing in an artful but friendly fashion, knowing the facts, getting a respectful hearing—but in the end not listened to.[17]

Even in his waning years, though, he kept up a lively correspondence with friends and with many inquirers. Toward his long-time theological adversaries, he took a decidedly conciliatory stance. When Paul Tillich said he'd be in the neighborhood and wanted to get together, Barth replied,

> Where shall we begin when we sit down together again? With the infirmities of age which obviously afflict us both? Or with the Ground of Being which unconditionally affects both of us? Or with your difficulty—I mean my own difficulty in reading your books? . . . Or with the question whether you will soon catch up with me in having a great-grandson?[18]

Emil Brunner, his early ally with whom he broke so decisively with his famous *Nein!*, was also growing old. Brunner's wife would write Barth to tell about her husband's declining condition. In one reply, Barth says,

> The fact was that God not only led him and me on very different paths, but in his unfathomable goodness and wisdom willed us already to be very different people—so different that properly there could be no question at all of strife or suffering between us. And yet we did strive and suffer on both sides. And if I am right he suffered more at my hands than I did at his, once I had let off steam in 1934.[19]

In another, he said,

> Your letter and the two appended lines by Emil touched me very much. Tell him the time is long past when I shout No to

him or anybody. We all can and should be glad to have a God who without any merits on our part says Yes to each of us in his own way.[20]

Though he was not able to answer all the inquiries he received for theological advice, he did try to answer many. Again his pastoral touch comes through time and again. One letter in particular shows his ability to be theological, pastoral, and personal at the same time. The writer had asked Barth, "Who (or what) is God for you?"

> I call this a good, short question. But I can give only a short and, I hope, good answer. First note two things:
>
> In no case is God a "what" that one may peep at close up or at a distance and value or disparage as one pleases. God is a "Who."
>
> And He is not who He is "for me" or "for you" (according to our ideas of Him) but in His own reality and truth, above both you and me, for all men, for the whole world. And hence also for you and for me.
>
> Who is God? I have no original answer to give you to this question, but can affirm Him only as He has shown and expressed Himself before us, apart from us, and therefore for us.
>
> Thus He is our, your and my, Creator and Lord, who judges and has mercy on us, our Father and Redeemer. It is thus that He revealed and reveals Himself in the history of Israel and in Jesus Christ, to which witness is given in Scripture. Think carefully about each of these words, yet not according to your own opinion, but as you try to read the Bible and pray a little. Each of these words is a pointer to God Himself.[21]

Death

Some sadness combined with wistfulness often characterized his last years. He did not like getting old, and he let his companions know it. "Lollo has told me plainly (apropos Job) that of all the men she has met I am the most unwilling to suffer," he wrote a friend.[22] And in another letter he admitted, "The only thing is that I have to combat an inexplicable sadness which all the successes life brought me can do nothing at all to allay."[23]

Many of his last birthdays were occasions for festschrifts, parties, commemorations, and the like. And Barth would pen a circular letter to the many who had wished him well. In his circular letter after his seventy-fifth birthday, he said he was grateful for the words of appreciation:

> Understandably this has moved me and comforted me, especially when pastors told me I gave them courage and joy in their preaching. But I can only pass on these thanks to Him to whom alone I myself owe each and every thing. Indeed I am sometimes frightened when I see the amount of free and unmerited grace that has ruled over and in my life, action, and work.
>
> It has been almost like something alien, in strange contrast to my own life day by day and year by year in which I have smoked my pipe and have sometimes indulged other appetites, and have rather wheezily thought and written and spoken what seemed to follow next, although always under the impression that I was some distance behind what was really happening.[24]

He recognized that many others worked just as hard if not harder than he did, and yet worked in relative obscurity. He said it was "pleasant" to be referred to as "the greatest scholar of all time," as the icing on one cake said. But, he asked, "Who will finally be praised?"

From the moment his star began to rise, Barth was never happy about the fact that there were Barthians. He was never interested in having people follow him. He wrote his theology, he said, as an attempt to think about Jesus Christ in the context of the challenges and problems of the day. He wanted to model a way of doing theology—grounded in the Bible—more than to champion a particular theology. So it's not surprising that at the end of this circular letter he said,

> I also admonish you in all seriousness, don't make a myth out of me, for the angels will certainly not like that and the perspicacious will see through it to my shame. Let each try to do what I have attempted, doing in his own field, better than I have done, a little something that will be to the glory of God and his neighbors. Until the third millennium comes (and beyond) there will be many, many new things in the church and in theology for those of true heart and good will to think and do.[25]

Barth wrote a few more circular letters, often making the same points. He died seven years after writing this one above, at the age of eighty-two, on December 9, 1968. He had been writing a lecture, and he broke off in mid-sentence and then went to bed, passing away peacefully in his sleep.

Since then, the third millennium has come, and indeed the church faces new and equally challenging times. Barth seems to have anticipated these times. One startling change that has occurred is the rise of worldwide Pentecostalism and a global awareness of the ministry of the Holy Spirit. Barth may have sensed this coming; he once said that if he were to start his *Dogmatics* again, he might very well make the center not the revelation of God in Jesus Christ but the work of the Holy Spirit.

Be that as it may, the point of learning about Barth and studying his theology is, as he said, not to create new Barthians. It is to watch him discover afresh the dynamic, powerful, gracious, and joyful good news of the gospel. And then it is to watch him, like John the Baptist in the famous Grünewald painting, point his finger "in an impossible way" to Jesus Christ.

CHAPTER 14

"Liberal" Evangelicalism?

*The efforts of Schleiermacher and his successors did not acquire
any significance for the broad mass of the "cultured" to whom
Schleiermacher addressed himself so impressively with his proof
of the roots of religion in the structure of man's spiritual life.*
— Karl Barth, "Evangelical Theology in the 19th Century"

Before we close this book, we should pause and note what nineteenth-century liberalism and modern evangelicalism have in common. Because what Barth was reacting against was, in many ways, similar to our situation today.

The assumption behind that sentence will surprise some. Modern evangelicalism has seen itself as a movement that is anything but liberal, that in fact repudiates liberalism. The magazine that was for decades the flagship of the movement, *Christianity Today*, was founded by Billy Graham as a foil to *The Christian Century*, a journal that epitomized liberalism.

In the 1950s, *The Christian Century* was the magazine of pastors in America. The optimism of nineteenth-century liberalism had been tempered by theologians such as Reinhold Niebuhr and Paul Tillich, who regularly appeared in the pages of the *Century*. But the *Century*'s liberalism still strongly permeated its pages. It showed confidence in reason and science to point the way forward in theology and human affairs. While recognizing the sinfulness

of humankind, it still featured pieces that assumed that, with education and ethical prodding, people could be persuaded to do the
right thing in their personal lives and in society. It was a magazine
that included articles pointing to the subjective nature of faith and
the historical and somewhat relative nature of Christianity as a
religion.

The Christian Century shared in the basic liberal assumptions
first outlined in the Enlightenment. As Gary Dorrien, author of *The
Making of American Liberal Theology: Idealism, Realism, and Modernity,
1900–1950*, puts it,

> The essential idea of liberal theology is that all claims to truth,
> in theology as in other disciplines, must be made on the basis
> of reason and experience, not by appeal to external authority.
> Christian Scripture may be recognized as spiritually authorita-
> tive within Christian experience, but its word does not settle or
> establish truth claims about matters of fact.[1]

In short, *The Christian Century* was representative of nineteenth-
century liberalism, chastened by two world wars, yes, but nonetheless decidedly liberal.

Graham, in reflecting on the state of affairs in the 1950s, believed that "thousands of young ministers are really in the evangelical camp in their theological thinking and evangelistic zeal." But
he was troubled that the major denominations and other church
organizations "are directed by extreme liberals." This liberal bias
was reinforced, he said, by, among other things, *The Christian Century*, which "for a long time . . . has been the voice of liberalism in
this country." He went on:

> While its circulation is small, its influence is tremendous. It is
> constantly quoted in *Time*, *Newsweek*, and other secular maga-
> zines and newspapers. Its intellectual popular journalism is a
> must for thousands of ministers each week. It influences re-

ligious thought more than any single factor in Protestantism today, in my opinion.

He concluded by saying, "At the moment, there is no evangelical paper that has the respect that can challenge it."

His solution followed: he proposed that a magazine be created that would consist of "hard-hitting editorials on current subjects—that these editorials be popular, well thought out journalism very much like *The Christian Century*—that we discuss current subjects very much as *The Christian Century* does [but] from the evangelical viewpoint." He wanted the magazine to become "a new strong vigorous voice to call us together that will have the respect of all evangelicals of all stripes within our major denominations."[2]

In *Christianity Today*'s first editorial, the contrast with liberalism was emphasized. It noted how "theological liberalism has failed to meet the moral and spiritual needs of the people." And in response, it announced, "*Christianity Today* is confident that the answer to the theological confusion existing in the world is found in Christ and the Scriptures." And "those who direct the editorial policy of *Christianity Today* unreservedly accept the complete reliability and authority of the written Word of God. It is their conviction that the Scriptures teach the doctrine of plenary inspiration."

In reasserting the priority of revelation over reason, it also took a swipe at science: "*Christianity Today* takes cognizance of the dissolving effect of modern scientific theory upon religion. To counteract this tendency, it will set forth the unity of the Divine revelation in nature and Scripture."[3]

There could be no greater contrast between the evangelicalism and liberalism of the 1950s, if Billy Graham and Carl Henry, the first editor of CT, are to be believed.

"Liberal" Evangelicalism

But of course things were not that simple. As noted, The Christian Century had been chastened by history into recognizing the ongoing reality of original sin and the need for faith not just in religion or religious experience but in the person of Jesus Christ. And Christianity Today, for all its emphasis on the objective and supreme authority of Scripture and the priority of evangelism, was trying to distance itself from fundamentalism by embracing science and scholarship, and by reaching out socially in ways fundamentalists found unacceptable. Still, all that being said, post–World War II evangelicalism saw itself as the antidote to liberalism.

Today, it is sometimes difficult to tell the difference between a liberal and an evangelical, and sometimes even between The Christian Century and Christianity Today! Many card-carrying evangelical scholars are happily published in the Century and even serve on the Century's editorial board. Social justice, formerly the domain of liberals, has become a distinctive emphasis of evangelicals. Historical biblical scholarship, once derided by evangelical scholars, now is warmly embraced by many who identify themselves as evangelicals. Theologically, of course, evangelical scholars still differ in crucial respects from their mainline and liberal colleagues.

It's at the level of church life that the distinction between the liberalism of Schleiermacher and the evangelical ethos seem to meld in uncomfortable ways. This point has been made by many theologians today, including Michael Horton and Darren Marks.[4] One particularly good summary is found in Good News for Anxious Christians: 10 Practical Things You Don't Have to Do, by Philip Cary, professor of philosophy at Eastern University. Cary asserts that evangelicalism has morphed into what he calls the "new evangelicalism." He argues that the new evangelicalism, for all intents and purposes, is a reincarnation of the theology of Schleiermacher.

Each chapter of Cary's book names one neo-evangelical idea that he believes is not only harmful to the life of faith but is a fundamentally liberal expression of faith—that is, it makes faith primarily about our religious experience.

For example, his opening chapter is "Why You Don't Have to Hear God's Voice in Your Heart." Cary begins by relating a paper one of his students wrote. It was a paper on "revelation," but what the student meant by that was grounded in misconstruing religion as feeling. The problem with "revelation," the student said, was that you couldn't really tell if it was God's voice that you were hearing. Cary realized the student wasn't talking about the revelation of God in Holy Scripture but about an inward voice or feeling. This is a misunderstanding of the doctrine of revelation, which in classic orthodoxy is about something that comes to us from outside of us—in particular in the person of Jesus Christ and in the Scriptures that God has inspired.[5]

This student inadvertently exposes the primary way many evangelicals try to discern God's will in their lives today. It's not a matter of reading Scripture and listening to its clear and objective commands: to pray, to love, to forbear, to spread the gospel. No modern evangelical would deny that these commands are to be obeyed. But these sorts of things do not interest us as much as the inner voice of God telling us what to do in particular circumstances.

This creates a special tension, as we wait for a "sense of the Spirit" about what we are supposed to do with our lives. We hesitate to move forward with a career because we do not "feel called." We drag out relationships because we don't "feel God's leading" to marry. We don't get involved in our church or community because we don't "sense God's direction" or don't "feel the gifting." Faith has to have this inner dynamic, we argue, otherwise we will revert to rote religion or formalism or even legalism.

This is driven home to me in conversations with evangelical friends. One young woman was asking me about a school that taught people how to experience the gifts of the Spirit, with a special emphasis on the more supernatural gifts: healing, prophecy, and tongues. I suggested that my concern with such schools is that they encourage people to try to have an experience of God. Instead, I said, we should be looking to Scripture, not to discover how to have a supernatural experience, but to discern who God is and how we are called to live.

My friend was unfazed: "But doesn't the Bible teach us to desire the gifts of the Holy Spirit?"

To be sure, desire and experience are part and parcel of the Christian life. But like many people of our time, this woman had a theological imagination limited—and, one might add, captivated—by a desire for experience.

This emphasis on experience is no more evident than in our weekly gathering. It used to be called worship, or the worship of God. Now people often refer to it as "the worship experience." The music—whether hymns or contemporary music—is designed less to teach and more to help us feel something spiritual. Whereas hymns put the emphasis on the words—with rich and thoughtful expressions of the faith—contemporary music is mostly about engendering praiseful feelings. Thus the use of beat-driven songs with simple lyrics that are repeated over and over.

Thus it is not surprising to see many individuals in worship seemingly lost in their own personal experience, eyes shut, hands lifted up, striving to feel something spiritual. One cannot judge what goes on in the heart at such a moment—such actions can also signal merely an attempt to concentrate in prayer. But given how we talk about worship as experience, how music is used mostly to create mood, how we evaluate services based on whether they have helped us feel close to God—it's only natural in such a setting that we will start to do things with our bodies to help us create a spiritual feeling. Because, we say, worship that does not also help us feel something spiritual is perhaps a signal that we are in a "dead church."

As I've suggested above, to be a Christian is to enjoy an experience of God: the joy of forgiveness; a sense of intimacy with God; moments when you do, in fact, hear God reveal his will to you in some specific circumstance; a prophetic word spoken in prayer; a healing. This is perhaps the greatest contribution the Pentecostal movement has made to the worldwide faith. Worship is more than correct liturgy. Prayer is more than beautiful and concise wording. Faith is more than formal assent to the Nicene Creed. The Christian life is more than obeying rules. When we "receive the Holy Spirit," it's not just an idea, but a living reality. It should not surprise us that this reality causes us to feel and experience extraordinary things.

But in many evangelical circles, we have begun to equate *our experience* of Christ with *the gospel*, and not something that comes as a result of the gospel. We give more authority to what happens inside us than to the clear, objective teaching of God's Word in Scripture. We think it more important that we feel forgiven inwardly than that we are actually forgiven on the cross. Many of us have become, in many respects, disciples of Schleiermacher, the great apostle of religious feeling. Schleiermacher has been born again in evangelicalism.

In addition, many in our movement have become disciples of Ritschl, who put the emphasis not on feeling so much as on doing, and who characterized the Christian life in terms of the kingdom of God. We see this among those who put Paul and his theology on the back burner and focus on Jesus and his preaching of the kingdom. They rightly repudiate a faith that revolves around personal forgiveness but does little to love the neighbor. They are keenly sensitive to the biblical commands to serve the "orphan and widow," the poor and socially rejected. They are very much committed to social justice—rescuing women from sexual trafficking, digging wells to bring clean water to African villages, cleaning up the environment, working for racial justice and reconciliation, and so forth. Such projects, after all, help incarnate God's love and kingdom life in this world. The Christian faith is nothing if it is not about doing good, helping others, and contributing to human flourishing.

Hopefully it will be a long time before Christians divorce faith from concrete expressions of love in the social sphere. Faith without works is indeed a contradiction. Still, it doesn't take a vivid imagination to see how easily such an emphasis can morph into the worst of nineteenth-century liberalism, with its overemphasis on what we do and its equation of the kingdom of God with the church's current social and political projects.

What unites those whose faith is about feeling and those whose faith is about doing is this: the temptation to make Christianity human-centered—anthropocentric—mostly concerned about what we feel and do and only secondarily concerned about who God is and what he has done.

Heeding Barth's Critique

God is not unimportant to us, far from it. As much as there are similarities between nineteenth-century liberalism and contemporary evangelicalism, contemporary evangelicals are hardly liberals. Our talk about religious feeling is mixed with more healthy theological talk. We can go on and on about "being led by the Lord" and in the next sentence defend biblical inerrancy as the only way to protect objective truth. We assume that if we're faithful enough we'll be able to clearly hear a voice from the Lord, but we remain deeply distrustful of the capacity of humans to do and be good.

The point is not to make a sweeping condemnation of evangelicalism, as if it were the epitome of nineteenth-century liberalism. The point is not to look to Barth as our theological savior. The point is to suggest that the theology Barth eventually found bankrupt, and so ardently battled, is a theology we understand and identify with at some level. That we imbibe it unthinkingly is a problem, because as Barth's theology demonstrates, it is an approach that brings with it a host of problems, problems that undermine not only the church's integrity but especially its evangelistic mission.

If evangelicals are true to their heritage, they will heed the analysis of Barth regarding nineteenth-century liberalism's failure to win people to Christ.

> The efforts of Schleiermacher and his successors did not acquire any significance for the broad mass of the "cultured" to whom Schleiermacher addressed himself so impressively with his proof of the roots of religion in the structure of man's spiritual life.[6]

Yet even Barth acknowledged that religious experience has a place in the Christian faith. So his theology is not so much a rejection of this dynamic aspect of faith, but a theology that can prevent feeling and mere ethics from taking over and sabotaging the church's mission.

For the first few years of his pastoral life, Barth too was a devoted disciple of Schleiermacher in some respects, and of Ritschl in others, and of liberalism in general. But as he preached week after week, and as events unfolded in Germany, he slowly began to see not only that liberalism "failed to meet the moral and spiritual needs of the people," as *Christianity Today*'s first editorial put it, but that it did not do justice to the remarkable message he was reading in the New Testament.

Barth, as much as any theologian today, can help evangelicals never forget that remarkable message.

Notes

Notes to the Introduction

1. *Karl Barth–Rudolf Bultmann Letters, 1922–1966*, ed. Bernd Jaspert, trans. and ed. Geoffrey W. Bromiley (Grand Rapids: Eerdmans, 1981), 105.

2. Karl Adam, *Das Hochland*, June 1926. Adam's remark is quoted by J. McConnachie, "The Teaching of Karl Barth," *Hibbert Journal* 25 (1926–27): 385, and by F. F. Bruce, *Tyndale New Testament Commentary on Romans* (Downers Grove: InterVarsity, 1985), 67.

3. Thomas F. Torrance, "Introduction," in *Karl Barth: Theology and Church: Shorter Writings, 1920–1928*, translated by Louise Pettibone Smith (1962; Eugene, OR: Wipf & Stock, 2015), 7.

4. Thomas F. Torrance, *Karl Barth: Biblical and Evangelical Theologian* (Edinburgh: T&T Clark, 1990), 133.

5. Letter to Pastor Ulrich Hedinger, June 6, 1962, in Karl Barth, *Letters, 1961–1968*, ed. Jürgen Fangmeier and Hinrich Stoevesandt, trans. and ed. Geoffrey W. Bromiley (Grand Rapids: Eerdmans, 1981), 48.

6. Herman Melville, *Moby Dick, or The Whale* (1851; Raleigh: Hayes Barton Press, 2007), 184.

7. *Conversations with John Updike*, ed. James Plath (Jackson: University Press of Mississippi, 1994), 102.

Notes to Chapter 1

1. Clifford Green, *Bonhoeffer: A Theology of Sociality*, rev. ed. (Grand Rapids: Eerdmans, 1999), 312.

2. Eberhard Bethge, *Dietrich Bonhoeffer: Theologian, Christian, Contemporary*, trans. Eric Mosbacher and others (London: St. James's Place, 1970), 49.

3. Bethge, *Dietrich Bonhoeffer*, 117.

4. Bonhoeffer quoted in Andreas Pangritz, *Karl Barth in the Theology of Dietrich Bonhoeffer*, trans. Barbara Rumscheidt and Martin Rumscheidt (Grand Rapids: Eerdmans, 2000), 31. I am indebted to Jeff McSwain's *Movements of Grace: The Dynamic Christo-realism of Barth, Bonhoeffer, and the Torrances* (Eugene, OR: Wipf & Stock, 2010) for pointing me to the quotes about Bonhoeffer and Barth.

5. Eberhard Busch, *Karl Barth and the Pietists: The Young Karl Barth's Critique of Pietism and Its Response* (Downers Grove: InterVarsity, 1990), 20.

6. Busch, *Karl Barth and the Pietists*, 21.

7. Busch, *Karl Barth and the Pietists*, 95.

8. Karl Barth, "The Strange New World of the Bible," in *The Word of God and the Word of Man*, trans. Douglas Horton (Gloucester, MA: Peter Smith, 1978), 46–47.

9. I'm depending here on the summary of Kevin Vanhoozer in "A Person of the Book?," in *Karl Barth and Evangelical Theology: Convergences and Divergences*, ed. Sung Wook Chung (Grand Rapids: Baker Academic, 2000), 28–30.

10. Vanhoozer, "A Person of the Book?," 29.

11. Part of Graham's evaluation of the first issue of *Christianity Today*, October 25, 1956; *Christianity Today* archives.

12. Letter to Geoffrey Bromiley, June 1, 1961, in Barth, *Letters, 1961–1968*, 7–8.

13. Michael Horton, "A Stony Jar: The Legacy of Karl Barth for Evangelical Theology," in *Engaging with Barth: Contemporary Evangelical Critiques* (New York: T&T Clark, 1980), 380.

14. William Evans, "Comments on Karl Barth, Bruce McCormack, and the Neo-Barthian View of Scripture," Reformation 21 website, December 2008: http://www.reformation21.org/articles/comments-on-karl-barth-bruce-mc cormack-and-the-neobarthian-view-of-scripture.php.

15. For more details of the incident, see Collin Hansen's "Gospel Talk: Entire Area Young Life Staff Out after Evangelism Mandate," *Christianity Today*, February 2008, posted online at http://www.christianitytoday.com/ct/2008 /february/1.13.html.

Notes to Chapter 2

1. Unless otherwise noted, facts and quotes in this chapter come from Eberhard Busch's *Karl Barth: His Life from Letters and Autobiographical Texts*, trans.

John Bowden (Philadelphia: Fortress, 1976), 1–32. Specific references to this volume will be noted only for extended quotes.

2. Busch, *Karl Barth and the Pietists*, 10–12.

3. Busch, *Karl Barth: His Life*, 9.

Notes to Chapter 3

1. Merriam-Webster online dictionary, http://www.merriam-webster.com /dictionary/juggernaut.

2. http://jameshannam.com/medievalscience.htm.

3. James Hannam, "Medieval Science, the Church and Universities," Bede's Library website, http://www.bede.org.uk/university.htm.

4. B. A. Gerrish, *A Prince of the Church: Schleiermacher and the Beginnings of Modern Theology* (Philadelphia: Fortress, 1984), 25.

5. Friedrich Schleiermacher, *On Religion: Speeches to Its Cultured Despisers* (New York: Harper & Row, 1958), 31.

6. Friedrich Schleiermacher, *The Christian Faith* (1838; Amazon Digital Services, 2010), location 1706.

7. Karl Barth, "Evangelical Theology in the 19th Century," in *The Humanity of God* (Louisville: Westminster John Knox, 1960), 21.

Notes to Chapter 4

1. Unless otherwise noted, facts and quotes in this chapter come from Eberhard Busch's *Karl Barth: His Life*, 54–105.

2. *Karl Barth–Rudolf Bultmann Letters, 1922–1966*, 154.

3. Bruce McCormack, *Karl Barth's Critically Realistic Dialectical Theology: Its Genesis and Development, 1909–1936* (Oxford: Clarendon, 1997), Kindle edition, location 1079.

4. McCormack, *Karl Barth's Critically Realistic Dialectical Theology*, locations 469–82.

5. McCormack, *Karl Barth's Critically Realistic Dialectical Theology*, location 1372.

6. McCormack, *Karl Barth's Critically Realistic Dialectical Theology*, locations 1372–73.

7. Barth, *Word of God, Word of Man*, 45.

8. McCormack, *Karl Barth's Critically Realistic Dialectical Theology*, locations 1620–21.

Notes to Chapter 5

1. Busch, *Karl Barth: His Life*, 113.

2. Busch, *Karl Barth: His Life*, 115.

3. Busch, *Karl Barth: His Life*, 110–11.

4. McCormack, *Karl Barth's Critically Realistic Dialectical Theology*, location 2722.

5. McCormack, *Karl Barth's Critically Realistic Dialectical Theology*, location 2104.

6. Busch, *Karl Barth: His Life*, 117.

7. Karl Barth, *The Epistle to the Romans*, trans. from the 6th ed. by Edwyn C. Hoskyns (Oxford: Oxford University Press, 1933), 15.

8. Barth, *Romans*, 7.

9. Barth, *Romans*, 44.

10. Busch, *Karl Barth: His Life*, 119.

11. Busch, *Karl Barth: His Life*, 119.

12. Barth, *Romans*, 56.

13. Barth, *Romans*, 57–58.

14. As quoted in McCormack, *Karl Barth's Critically Realistic Dialectical Theology*, location 2786, who translated this from the 1922 edition of *Der Römerbrief*, 213.

15. Barth, *Romans*, 31.

16. Barth, *Romans*, 39.

17. Barth, *Romans*, 330–31.

18. Barth, *Romans*, 63.

19. Barth, *Romans*, 151.

20. Barth, *Romans*, 69–70.

Notes to Chapter 6

1. Barth, *Romans*, 335.

2. Barth, *Romans*, 136.

3. Barth, *Romans*, 136.

4. Barth, *Romans*, 334.

5. Barth, *Romans*, 335.

6. As quoted in McCormack, *Karl Barth's Critically Realistic Dialectical Theology*, location 2611.

7. Barth, *Romans*, 314–15.

8. Barth, *Romans*, 151.

9. Barth, *Word of God, Word of Man*, 186.

10. Barth, *Romans*, 31, 39, 70, respectively.

11. Barth, *Romans*, 39.

12. Barth, *Romans*, 49.

13. Barth, *Romans*, 35.

14. Barth, *Romans*, 114.

15. Busch, *Karl Barth: His Life*, 110.

16. Busch, *Karl Barth: His Life*, 121.

Notes to Chapter 7

1. Busch, *Karl Barth: His Life*, 124. I'm indebted to pages 124–89 in Busch's volume for much of the narrative of this chapter.

2. Busch, *Karl Barth: His Life*, 126.

3. Busch, *Karl Barth: His Life*, 116.

4. McCormack, *Karl Barth's Critically Realistic Dialectical Theology*, location 3316.

5. McCormack, *Karl Barth's Critically Realistic Dialectical Theology*, location 3325.

6. McCormack, *Karl Barth's Critically Realistic Dialectical Theology*, location 3338.

7. McCormack, *Karl Barth's Critically Realistic Dialectical Theology*, location 3356.

8. McCormack, *Karl Barth's Critically Realistic Dialectical Theology*, location 3370.

9. McCormack, *Karl Barth's Critically Realistic Dialectical Theology*, location 3379.

10. McCormack, *Karl Barth's Critically Realistic Dialectical Theology*, location 3401.

11. McCormack, *Karl Barth's Critically Realistic Dialectical Theology*, location 3397.

12. Busch, *Karl Barth: His Life*, 138.

13. D. Densil Morgan, *The SPCK Introduction to Karl Barth* (London: SPCK, 2010), 35.

14. Busch, *Karl Barth: His Life*, 155.

15. Morgan, *SPCK Introduction to Karl Barth*, 36.
16. Morgan, *SPCK Introduction to Karl Barth*, 36.
17. Busch, *Karl Barth: His Life*, 138.
18. Morgan, *SPCK Introduction to Karl Barth*, 39.
19. Busch, *Karl Barth: His Life*, 186.

Notes to Chapter 8

1. Busch, *Karl Barth: His Life*, 221–22. The narrative of this chapter is indebted to pages 216–34 in Busch's volume. Specific references to this volume will be given only for extended quotes.
2. As found in McCormack, *Karl Barth's Critically Realistic Dialectical Theology*, location 4705.
3. Busch, *Karl Barth: His Life*, 218.
4. J. S. Conway, *The Nazi Persecutions of the Churches, 1933–34* (Vancouver, BC: Regent College Publishing, 1968), 20.
5. James A. Zabel, *Nazism and the Pastors: A Study of the Ideas of Three Deutsche Christen Groups* (Missoula: Scholars, 1976), 28.

Notes to Chapter 9

1. Busch, *Karl Barth: His Life*, 232. The narrative of this chapter is grounded in pages 227–62 in Busch's volume. Specific references to this volume will be given only for extended quotes.
2. Renate Wind, *Dietrich Bonhoeffer: A Spoke in the Wheel* (Grand Rapids: Eerdmans, 1992), 76–77.
3. Busch, *Karl Barth: His Life*, 242–43.
4. Arthur C. Cochrane, *The Church's Confession under Hitler* (Philadelphia: Westminster, 1962), 239.
5. Cochrane, *The Church's Confession under Hitler*, 241.

Notes to Chapter 10

1. This chapter is essentially a thematic summary of Barth's life from 1935 to about 1962 as examined by Busch in *Karl Barth: His Life*, 263–456. Only extended quotes are individually referenced.
2. Busch, *Karl Barth: His Life*, 272–73.
3. Busch, *Karl Barth: His Life*, 274.

4. Busch, *Karl Barth: His Life*, 315.

5. Busch, *Karl Barth: His Life*, 290.

6. Busch, *Karl Barth: His Life*, 305.

7. Busch, *Karl Barth: His Life*, 318.

8. Busch, *Karl Barth: His Life*, 323.

9. Karl Barth, *Church Dogmatics in Outline* (New York: Harper & Row, 1959), 7.

10. Busch, *Karl Barth: His Life*, 358.

11. Busch, *Karl Barth: His Life*, 282.

12. Busch, *Karl Barth: His Life*, 357.

13. Busch, *Karl Barth: His Life*, 383.

14. Estimates range widely, and these numbers represent a middle position among historians. A good summary of the leading arguments for each can be found at https://en.wikipedia.org/wiki/Joseph_Stalin#Calculating_the _number_of_victims.

15. Busch, *Karl Barth: His Life*, 431.

16. Busch, *Karl Barth: His Life*, 375.

17. Busch, *Karl Barth: His Life*, 388.

18. Busch, *Karl Barth: His Life*, 414.

Notes to Chapter 11

1. See Geoffrey W. Bromiley, *Introduction to the Theology of Karl Barth* (Edinburgh: T&T Clark, 1979).

2. Busch, *Karl Barth: His Life*, 210.

3. Karl Barth, *Church Dogmatics*, 14 vols., 2nd ed., ed. G. W. Bromiley and T. F. Torrance, trans. G. W. Bromiley (Edinburgh and New York: T&T Clark, 1975–), I/1, 112.

4. *Church Dogmatics*, I/1, 110.

5. *Church Dogmatics*, I/1, 109.

6. As quoted by Vanhoozer, "A Person of the Book?," 30–31.

7. John Webster, *Karl Barth* (London: Continuum, 2000), 65.

8. *Church Dogmatics*, I/1, 463.

9. Vanhoozer, "A Person of the Book?," 42.

10. Quoted in Vanhoozer, "A Person of the Book?," 45.

11. Vanhoozer, "A Person of the Book?," 43.

12. Karl Barth, *An Introduction to Evangelical Theology* (New York: Doubleday Anchor Books, 1964), 31.

Notes to Chapter 12

1. *Church Dogmatics*, IV/1, 630.

2. *Church Dogmatics*, IV/1, 515.

3. *Church Dogmatics*, IV/1, 477.

4. *Church Dogmatics*, IV/1, 477.

5. Hans Urs von Balthasar, *The Theology of Karl Barth*, trans. Edward T. Oakes (San Francisco: Ignatius, 1992), 186.

6. Oliver Crisp, "On Barth's Denial of Universalism," *Themelios* 29 (2003): 18–29.

7. George Hunsinger, *How to Read Karl Barth: The Shape of His Theology* (New York: Oxford University Press, 1991), 108.

8. *Church Dogmatics*, IV/1, 568.

9. Hunsinger's discussion is found in *How to Read Karl Barth*, 106–9. Thanks to Christopher Benson for helping me summarize this complex discussion and pointing me to key passages in Hunsinger.

10. The following summary and quotes come from Jeff McSwain's essay "Young Life and the Gospel of All-Along Belonging," The Other Journal .com, http://theotherjournal.com/2010/01/06/young-life-and-the-gospel-of -all-along-belonging/.

Notes to Chapter 13

1. Thomas Oden, *The Promise of Karl Barth: The Ethics of Freedom* (New York: Lippincott, 1969), 16.

2. John Updike, "Foreword" in Karl Barth, *Wolfgang Amadeus Mozart*, trans. Clarence K. Pott (Grand Rapids: Eerdmans, 1986), 7.

3. Busch, *Karl Barth: His Life*, 220.

4. Letter to Max Zellweger, April 18, 1962, in Barth, *Letters, 1961–1968*, 44.

5. Letter to Max Zellweger, May 19, 1962, in Barth, *Letters, 1961–1968*, 43.

6. Busch, *Karl Barth: His Life*, 121.

7. Busch, *Karl Barth: His Life*, 164.

8. "Who Said What about Karl Barth?" Center for Barth Studies, Princeton Theological Seminary. http://barth.ptsem.edu/.

9. Busch, *Karl Barth: His Life*, 235.

10. Busch, *Karl Barth: His Life*, 399.

11. Karl Barth, "Saved by Grace," August 14, 1955, in *Deliverance to the Captives* (New York: Harper & Brothers, 1961), 35–42.

12. Charles M. Cameron, "Karl Barth the Preacher," *Evangelical Quarterly* 66, no. 2 (1994): 106.

13. Barth, "Saved by Grace," 35.

14. Cameron, "Karl Barth the Preacher," 100.

15. Busch, *Karl Barth: His Life*, 244.

16. Circular letter of May 1961, in Barth, *Letters, 1961–1968*, 4.

17. Letter to Helmut Gollwitzer, July 31, 1962, in Barth, *Letters, 1961–1968*, 61.

18. Letter to Paul Tillich, November 22, 1963, in Barth, *Letters, 1961–1968*, 142.

19. Letter to Margrit Brunner, April 16, 1966, in Barth, *Letters, 1961–1968*, 204.

20. Letter to Margrit Brunner, March 7, 1966, in Barth, *Letters, 1961–1968*, 200.

21. Letter to N.N., in Barth, *Letters, 1961–1968*, 55–56.

22. Letter to Ernst Wolf, November 8, 1962, in Barth, *Letters, 1961–1968*, 74.

23. Letter to Margrit Bruner, March 7, 1966, in Barth, *Letters, 1961–1968*, 27.

24. Circular letter of May 1961, in Barth, *Letters, 1961–1968*, 3–4.

25. Circular letter of May 1961, in Barth, *Letters, 1961–1968*, 4.

Notes to Chapter 14

1. Gary Dorrien, *The Making of American Liberal Theology: Idealism, Realism, and Modernity, 1900–1950* (Louisville: Westminster John Knox, 2003), 1.

2. From a speech given by Billy Graham in 1955. From the *Christianity Today* archives.

3. *Christianity Today* 1, no. 1 (October 15, 1956): 20–23.

4. See especially Michael Horton's *Christless Christianity: The Alternative Gospel of the American Church* (Grand Rapids: Baker, 2008), and Darren Marks, "The Mind under Grace: Why Theology Is an Essential Nutrient for Spiritual Growth," *Christianity Today* 54, no. 3 (March 2010): 23–27.

5. Philip Cary, *Good News for Anxious Christians: 10 Practical Things You Don't Have to Do* (Grand Rapids: Brazos, 2010), 1–2.

6. Barth, "Evangelical Theology in the 19th Century," 21.

Annotated Bibliography

Having read Barth and about Barth since seminary, I can't possibly recall all the books and articles that have influenced the writing of this book. But the following are the ones I relied on most recently. Double asterisks (**) point to recommended reading for those just beginning to explore Barth.

Books by Karl Barth

The Church Dogmatics. 14 volumes. 2nd edition. Edited by G. W. Bromiley and T. F. Torrance. Translated by G. W. Bromiley. Edinburgh and New York: T&T Clark, 1975–.

– Barth's central work, but I wouldn't recommend beginning here. This is technical theology, and while some passages soar and inspire, large sections are written for professional theologians.

Deliverance to the Captives. Translated by Marguerite Wieser. New York: Harper & Brothers, 1961.

– A collection of sermons that Barth preached to Basel prisoners. They give a good sense of how Barth spoke to "common people" about the faith.

***Dogmatics in Outline*. Translated by G. T. Thomson. New York: Harper Perennial, 1959.

— Barth's commentary on the Apostles' Creed. It presents the major themes of his theology in an accessible manner. If one has time for only one Barth book, this would be the one to read.

The Epistle to the Romans. Translated from the 6th edition by Edwyn C. Hoskyns. London: Oxford University Press, 1972.

— Not an easy work, but I still recommend it. I've read it three or four times now, and each time it gets a little easier! To be sure, Barth criticized himself for overstatement in this book, but watching as he discovers that God is God and all that implies is thrilling.

***Evangelical Theology: An Introduction*. Translated by Grover Foley. Grand Rapids: Eerdmans, 1963.

— Barth's lectures on what it means to be an evangelical (that is, Protestant) theologian. Here Barth's joy and confidence in the gospel shine.

The Humanity of God. Translated by Thomas Weiser and John Newton Thomas. Louisville: Westminster John Knox, 1960.

— A short work, composed of three lectures given later in life.

Learning Jesus Christ through the Heidelberg Catechism. Translated by Shirley Guthrie. Grand Rapids: Eerdmans, 1964.

— Barth's commentary on the famous catechism.

Letters, 1961–1968. Edited by Jürgen Fangmeier and Hinrich Stoevesandt. Translated and edited by Geoffrey W. Bromiley. Grand Rapids: Eerdmans, 1981.

– Fascinating excerpts from letters to family and friends in his last years.

The Word of God and the Word of Man. Translated by Douglas Horton. Gloucester, MA: Peter Smith, 1978.

– Lectures Barth gave as he was being converted away from liberalism.

Books about Barth and His Theology

Balthasar, Hans Urs von. *The Theology of Karl Barth*. Translated by Edward T. Oakes. San Francisco: Ignatius, 1951, 1992.

– The famous Catholic theologian's take on Barth. His major thesis has since been challenged by McCormack, but this book remains an important summary of Barth's views on many topics.

Bromiley, Geoffrey W. *Introduction to the Theology of Karl Barth*. Edinburgh: T&T Clark, 1979.

– Bromiley, who translated Barth's *Dogmatics*, outlines the content of each volume, with very little comment. A dry read, but helpful to get an overview.

Busch, Eberhard. *Karl Barth and the Pietists: The Young Karl Barth's Critique of Pietism and Its Response*. Translated by Donald W. Bloesch. Downers Grove: InterVarsity, 2004.

– Pietist blood runs through evangelicals' veins, so this study sheds a lot of light on what Barth might think of evangelicals today!

Busch, Eberhard. *Karl Barth: His Life from Letters and Autobiographical Texts*. Translated by John Bowden. 2nd edition. Philadelphia: Fortress, 1976.

– This is the most thorough biography of Barth available. It is an absolutely indispensable resource for anyone who wants to understand Barth. But it records life only from Barth's perspective, so we still await a definitive biography that relies on sources other than Barth himself.

Busch, Eberhard. *The Great Passion: An Introduction to Karl Barth's Theology.* Translated by Geoffrey W. Bromiley. Grand Rapids: Eerdmans, 1964.

– Barth's biographer and one-time assistant outlines the themes of Barth. One of the better summaries, but still a challenging read.

Cary, Philip. *Good News for Anxious Christians.* Grand Rapids: Brazos, 2010.

– Not about Barth as such, but a helpful analysis of contemporary evangelicalism that resonates with much of Barth's emphases, though Cary himself is a Lutheran.

Cochrane, Arthur C. *The Church's Confession under Hitler.* Philadelphia: Westminster, 1962.

– A history of the Confessing Church in 1930s Germany.

Franke, John. *Barth for Armchair Theologians.* Louisville: Westminster John Knox, 2006.

– An introductory biography that spends more time on theology than does the present one.

Chung, Sung Wook, editor. *Karl Barth and Evangelical Theology: Convergences and Divergences.* Grand Rapids: Baker Academic, 2006.

– Evangelical theologians respond to Barth on various themes. As with any collection of essays, some are better than others.

Gibson, David, and Daniel Strange, editors. *Engaging with Barth: Contemporary Evangelical Critiques*. New York: T&T Clark, 2008.

– Again, evangelical theologians respond to Barth on various themes.

Horton, Michael. *Christless Christianity: The Alternative Gospel of the American Church*. Grand Rapids: Baker, 2008.

– Not a book about Barth but an analysis of evangelical culture that suggests how "liberal" segments of evangelicals have become.

**Hunsinger, George. *How to Read Karl Barth: The Shape of His Theology*. New York: Oxford University Press, 1991.

– The opening section of this book is indispensable for reading Barth. Hunsinger describes six motifs that are found in Barth's theology—actualism, particularism, objectivism, personalism, realism, and rationalism—motifs that go a long way toward helping the reader grasp a Barthian argument.

Mangina, Joseph L. *Karl Barth: Theologian of Christian Witness*. Louisville: Westminster John Knox, 2004.

– An introductory overview of Barth's theology.

McCormack, Bruce L. *Karl Barth's Critically Realistic Dialectical Theology: Its Genesis and Development, 1909–1936*. Oxford: Clarendon, 1997.

– A technical work of theology in parts, but it contains some fascinating background, especially to Barth's writing of *Romans*.

McSwain, Jeff. *Movements of Grace: The Dynamic Christo-realism of Barth, Bonhoeffer, and the Torrances*. Eugene, OR: Wipf & Stock, 2010.

– The former Young Life leader outlines the theology that now drives his evangelistic ministry to youth.

Migliore, Daniel L., editor. *Reading the Gospels with Karl Barth*. Grand Rapids: Eerdmans, 2017.

– The essays discuss the many things Barth had to say about the Gospels throughout the *Dogmatics*. A nice way to get into the *Dogmatics*.

Morgan, D. Densil. *The SPCK Introduction to Karl Barth*. London: SPCK, 2010.

– Another fine introductory biography of Barth, with a good summary of the *Church Dogmatics*.

**Webster, John. *Barth*. London: Continuum, 2000.

– An introductory overview of Barth's theology in its various stages.

**Willimon, William. *Conversations with Barth on Preaching*. Nashville: Abingdon, 2006.

– This volume tends to ramble, but it's the ramblings that I find most interesting. Reflecting on Barth in respect to preaching keeps the conversation grounded in the realities of church life. I find this a great way to think about Barth's theology.

Willimon, William. *The Early Preaching of Karl Barth: Fourteen Sermons with Commentary*. Louisville: Westminster John Knox, 2009.

– The Methodist bishop and preacher has long been an appreciative student of Barth and his preaching. This book takes a look at Barth's sermons as he was moving toward historic orthodoxy.

Magazine and Web Resources and Occasional Essays

Two websites that host a variety of resources on Barth are found at:

- Princeton Theological Seminary:http://barth.ptsem.edu/
- Tyndale Seminary:http://www.tyndale.ca/seminary/mtsmodu lar/reading-rooms/theology/barth

Two essays on the Theophilogue website provide helpful summaries of Barth's theology of election:

- "How Barth's Doctrine of Election Informs His Doctrine of Justification," http://theophilogue.wordpress.com/2009/03 /07/how-barths-doctrine-of-election-informs-his-doctrine-of -justification/
- "Did Barth Teach Contingent or Necessary Universalism?" http://theophilogue.wordpress.com/2009/03/11/did-karl -barth-teach-contingent-or-necessary-universalism/

To see how one blogger tries to mine the theology of Karl Barth and T. F. Torrance for both theology and ministry, see The Evangelical Calvinist: https://growrag.wordpress.com/.

Another helpful essay posted on-line is "Young Life and the Gospel of All-Along Belonging" by Jeff McSwain, The Other Journal .com, http://theotherjournal.com/2010/01/06/young-life-and-the -gospel-of-all-along-belonging/.

I culled many evangelical observations about Barth from the archives of *Christianity Today*, starting with the first issue, October 15, 1956. Those archives will be available electronically in the next few years.

Index